DAVNGEROVS POSITIONS AND PROCEEDINGS, published and practised within this Iland of *Brytaine*, *under pretence of Reformation*, *and for the Presbiteriall Discipline*.

DAVNGEROVS POSITIONS AND PROCEEDINGS, published and practised within this Iland of *Brytaine, under pretence of Reformation, and for the Presbiteriall Discipline.*

Δεινὰ τὰ τῶν τυραννῶν λήμματα.

My sonne feare the Lord and the King : and meddle not with them that are seditious. *Prou. 24. 21.*

They despise gouernement, and speake euill of them that are in authority. *Iude.*

LONDON
Imprinted by Iohn Wolfe.
1593.

S. B. N. - GB: 576.78308.0

Republished in 1968 by Gregg International Publishers Limited
1 Westmead, Farnborough, Hants., England

Printed in Germany

An aduertisement to the Reader.

THE *Author of this Treatise was required by some persons of honer, who might dispose of him and his labours: to set downe by way of an historicall narration, what hee had obserued touching certaine positions holden, and some enterprises atchieued or vndertaken, for recommending, and bringing the* Presbiteriall *D*iscipline *into this Iland of* Brittaine, *vnder pretence of reformation. The performance of which dutie, when hee had vndertaken and was entred into it: hee found the worke to grow farre greater vpon him, then at the first, he did imagine, Insomuch as although in the beginning he verily supposed, tha hee might easily haue contriued his matter into a few sheetes of paper: so that as many coppies, as were to bee disposed, might easily and in very short time haue beene written forth: yet by the necessary length of the Discourse, as it fell out, and through his manifold quotations, hee was constrained, (as the time required) to procure for the better dispatch, that some fewe copies might bee printed. And albeit there is no meaning, that this Treatise (laboured but for the priuate satisfaction of some fewe especiall persons) should otherwise continue then as an vnpublished Copie: yet the writer of it wished to haue it signified, that nothing is alleadged therein, which is not to be found either in Bookes and writinges published to the view of the world, (such as he thinketh will not be disclaimed,) or in publike records, or else is to be shewed vnder those parties own hands that haue beene either the principall procurers, fauorers, or dealers in those thinges, whereof hee intreateth. Which asseueration of his thus made, he will be ready, (as he sayth) God assisting him, to iustifie at any time for the satisfaction of such, as shall make doubt of it. And doth further protest with all sinceritie: that he hath not (willingly) detorted any thing in this whole Discourse, to make either the cause it selfe, or the fauorors thereof more odious, then their owne wordes and deeds shall necessarily inferre, and enforce against them, with all indifferent and considerate Readers.* Farewell in Christ.

The Contents of the first Booke.

The Contents of the second Booke.

Some

The Contents of the third Booke.

FINIS.

Thou ſhalt not rayle vpon the Iudges, *neither ſpeake euill of the Ruler of the people.* Exod.22.28.

The Lord keepe mee from laying my hand on him. For hee is the Lordes annointed. 1.King.24.

Who can lay his handes vpon the Lordes annointed, and bee guiltleſſe? 1.King.26.

Speake not euil of the King: no, not in thy thought. Eccle. 20.

Let euery ſoule bee ſubiect to the higher powers: for there is no power but of God: and the powers that bee, are ordayned of God. Whoſoeuer therefore reſiſteth the power, reſiſteth the ordinance of God: and they that reſiſt ſhall receiue to themſelues iudgement. Ye muſt be ſubiect, not becauſe of wrath onely, but alſo for conſcience ſake. Paule to the Rom.13.

We call vpon the euerlaſting God for the health of our Emperors, alwaies beſeeching Almighty God, to ſend euery of them long life, happy raigne, truſtie ſeruantes, valiant ſouldiers, faithfull Councellors, orderly Subiectes, and the world quiet: and whatſoeuer people or Prince can wiſh for. Tertul. in Apologetico.

One night with a few firebrandes, would yeald vs reuenge ſufficient, if it were lawfull with vs to requite euill with euill. But God forbid, that eyther they, which take part with God, ſhould reuenge themſelues with humaine fire, or bee grieued to ſuffer wherein they be tried. If wee would not practiſe ſecrete reuenge, but profeſſe open enmity, could we lacke number of men or force of Armes? Are the Moores *thinke you or the* Parthians, *or any one Nation whatſoeuer, moe in number then we, that are ſpread ouer the whole world? We are not of you, and yet wee haue filled all the places and roomes which you haue: your Cities, Ilandes, Caſtles, Townes, Aſſemblies, your Tentes, Tribes, and Wardes, yea the very Palace, Senate, and Iudgement ſeates. For what* Tertul. in Apologet.

war

warre were wee not able and readie, though wee were fewer in number then you, that go to our deathes so gladly, if it were not more lawfull in our religion to be slaine then to slay? We coulde without armes neuer rebelling, but onely diuiding our selues from you, haue done you spight inough with that seperation. For if so greate a multitude as we are, should haue broken from you, into some corner of the world, the losse of so many CitiZens woulde haue both shamed you, and punished you. Belieue me, you would haue been afraide, to see your selues alone and amaZed as amongst the dead, to see silence and desolation euery where, you would haue had moe enemies, then inhabitantes, where now you haue fewer ennemies, by reason of the multitude of your Citizens, that are almost all Christians.

August. con. .lit. Petil. lib. 2 cap. 48.

Saul *had not innocencie, and yet hee had holynes, not of life, but of vnction.*

Chrisost. de verb. Esa. vidi dominum.

After the Priest had reproued the attempt, and the king would not yeeld, but offred Armes, shieldes, and speares, and vsed his power: then the Priest turning himselfe to God: I haue done (saith he) my duty to warne him, I can goe no further. For it is the Priests part onely to reproue, & freely to admonish (with words,) not to assaile with arms, not to vse targets, not to handle speares, not to bend bowes, nor to cast dartes, but onely to reproue and freely to warne.

Hit. lib. 2. adu. Iouinianum.

Pateat quod noxium est, vt possit conteri cum patuerit.

THE

THE FIRST BOOKE OF DISCIPLINARY GROVNDES and Practises.

Chap. I.

Of two sortes of men that especially disturbe the Church of England, and of the drifts of them both, by way of a Preface.

S it is said of *Caiphas*, when hee tolde his companions the Pharisees and the rest, that it was expedient for them, that *one man should die for the people, Hoc a seipso non dixit, sed prophetauit, &c.* so in mine opinion it may well be said of the Pope, when he gaue to the Kings & Queenes of England this Title, to bee called *Defenders of the faith*: he spake not this of himselfe, but prophecied. For if any Christian King or Queene might euer bee truely so tearmed, (as in deed it is a stile that containeth a great and the most royall part of all their kingly offices,) surely of all the Princes that since that time haue raigned, it is verified most properly in her most excellent Maiestie: Whether you respect the Reformation of Religion, which her Highnesse hath made in this Church of England (according to the noble examples of *Moses, Iosua, Dauid, Salomon, Iosaphat, Ezechias, Iosias, &c.*) or whether you respect, not onely the reliefe, which strangers persecuted at home for the profession of the Gospell haue here receiued: or her Maiesties great and vnspeakeable charges, for the ayding and assisting of other Christian States, Princes, and countries: that for their profession of the same right Religion, are mightily afflicted, by certaine Gyantes of the earth, the souldiers and members of that Antichrist of *Rome*.

So as in these and many other respects (which do concurre with them) I neither doubt that her Maiesty (whom the Lord protect with his mighty hande long to raigne ouer vs) shall bee for euer renowned amongst the most famous Queenes, that euer liued in the worlde: or that the Church of England, so refourmed by her Highnesse, is presently at this day the most Apostolike and flourishinge Church, simply, that is in all Christendome. Howbeit let a Church be as richly planted as euer any was, before, or in the Apostles times: Let either *Moses* with his *Aaron*, or *Dauid* with all his Councellors, gouerne both the Church and Common-wealth, as godly as euer any was gouerned: yet such is, and euer hath been, the malice and cunning of Sathan: as that he wanteth not at any time, either will or meanes, to slaunder, to depraue, and to endanger the same. He hath his *Core*, *Dathan*, and *Abiram*, that
Numb,16 if need bee, dare presume to tell both *Moses* and *Aaron*, they take too much vpon them. Hee is able to set the children of one father, the seruants of one master, the subiects of one Prince, and the members of one Church; at dissention, at deadly hatred amongst themselues. As occasion serueth, hee hath his *Shemeis* to curse King *Dauid*, also his
2,Sam,16 murmurers, complayners, mockers, makers of sectes, such as *despise gouernement*, which are presumptuous: men that
Iude
2,Pet,2 stand in their lewde conceits: such as feare not to speak euill of those things they know not, and of them that are in dignity, that is, of Princes and great men, be they neuer so high in authority.

The experience which wee haue hereof at this day in the Church of England, is more then pregnant: partly through the diuelish and traiterous practises of the Seminary Priests and Iesuites: and partly by reason of the lewd and obstinate course, held by our pretended refourmers, the Consistorian Puritanes: both of them labouring with all their might, by rayling, libelling, and lying, to steale away the peoples harts from their gouernours, to bringe them to a dislike of the present state of our Church, and to drawe them into parts-taking: the one sort, for the embracing of such directiõs, as should come vnto them from *Rome:* the other for the establishing of that counterfeit and false Hierarchie, which they would obtrude vppon vs by the countenance and name of the Church at *Geneua.*

The which proceedings of both the sorts of disturbers, are so much the more dangerous, in that they deale so secretely, and haue combined themselues, together with their Proselites, into such a league aud confederacy; as get out what you can your selfe by meere chance (as they say) for the discouery of their actions, and attempts; you shall bee sure that neither the one sort nor the other will detect any thing. Nay matters beeing detected in some sort to their handes, they will vtterly refuse to bee examined, as law prescribeth: or if they take any oathe, it is as good neuer a whit as neuer the better, they dally so exceedingly with it.

For vnder pretence of not accusing themselues, if they finde any thing to be come to light, which may any waies touch them, they will vtterly refuse for the most part to answere it, either vpon oath or without oath: saying, that neither by the Lawes of God, nor man, they are bound so to answere. Vnder colour whereof they exempt themselues from the ordinary course helde in iustice, for criminall causes, throughout all the world: which is, that before witnesses be produced against any supposed offender, the party accused shall first answere to the accusation, yea, or nay, &c. as wee vse in England, and that in matters of life and death (but in these without an oathe) hee must first pleade guilty or not guilty.

And as they deale for themselues,so doo they for their confederates,their fauourers,relieuers,abetters,and receiuers: affirming it to be against the rules of charity,to bring their Christian brethren and frends into any daunger,for doing of those things, which both the sorts of these seducers haue drawne them into,and doo themselues iudge to be religious and iust.

From these points all the Iudges of the land,and diuers Diuines that haue dealte with them, as yet cannot bringe them: both the sorts are so setled in this seditious doctrine of *Rhemes*, which is as followeth,vz. *If thou be put to an oath, to accuse Catholikes,for seruing God as they ought to doo,or to vtter any innocent man,to Gods enemies and his; thou oughtest first to refuse such vnlawfull oathes: but if thou haue not constancie, and courage so to doo,yet know thou that such oathes binde not at all in conscience and law of God, but may and must be broken vnder paine of damnation.*

Annotat. Rhemish vpon the 23. of the Actes of the Apostles.

Now in these confederacies,what course should be taken for the preuenting of such daungers, as may thereby ensue,I referre it to be throughly considered by those that haue the gouernement both of the Church and Common-weale committed vnto them. But before they can be preuented they must be vnderstood. Concerning the Seminary Priests and Iesuites: their very comming into the land doth declare their traiterous intentions. What alleageance and loue soeuer they pretend (vppon their apprehension) to her Maiesty and their countrey, it is very well knowne, they doo it but for the time, *rebus sic stantibus*, & that their comming hether, is to no other purpose, but to make a way for the Pope and the Spaniardes; the sworne and mortall enemies, both to this state, and to all other

that

that doo professe the right refourmed religion of Christ.

But for the other sort of practitioners, their proceedings and designements, are not so well, as yet discouered. Their pretences doo carry a greater shew of good meanings: & many (that are indeede truely zealous, little suspecting what hookes doo lie hidde vnder such faire baites) are dayly carried (as we see) headlong with them. In respect whereof, you are to be aduertised, that as it is an easie matter by looking to the said Popish and Spanish practises, to knowe in generality, their Seminaries dealinges here amongst vs, be they in particularity neuer so secrete: so are there certaine men in other countries, of the same humors with our pretended refourmers, whose courses and proceedings, as wel for the matters they desire, as for the manner of attaining of them, they propound to themselues, as the fittest patternes for them to followe: and namely the Ministers of *Geneua*, but more especially some of the Ministers of *Scotland*: as may hereby appeare.

As we haue beene an example, to the Churches of France *and* Scotland (sayth M. Cartwright) *to followe vs; so the Lorde would haue vs also to profite, and be prouoked by their example.* An other also in this sort. *Nobiles quidam pr*æ*cipui huius regni mecum egerunt, vt author essem regi meo de tollendis omninò Episcopatibus, vt exemplum posteà posset manare in vicinam Angliam. Certaine of the chiefe Noble men of England* (who I thinke nowe are gone,) *dealt with mee* (by the instigation no doubt of some of our Ministers, Anno, 1583.) *to persuade the King of* Scotland *my maister, to ouerthrowe all the Bishopprickes in his countrey, that his proceedinges therein might bee an example for* England *adioyning.* A Letter of P.A.

Vpon a certaine repaire of tenne thousand in armes to the King of Scots at *Sterling*, Anno, 1585. whereupon the Bishopprickes were indeed suppressed, *Knewstubbe* a Consistorian Knewstubbe.

ſiſtorian Miniſter of Suffolke, did write thus to *Fielde: I would bee glad to heare ſomewhat of the eſtate of* Scotland: *it doth more trouble me then our owne: For I am conceiuing ſome hope vpon the change of their former proceeding.*

It alſo appeareth that there is great and ordinary intelligence, betwixt their and our eſpeciall presbyterie miniſters, for the better, and more ready compaſſing of ſuch deuiſes and platformes, as are ſought for, by our ſaid miniſters ſo buſily amongſt vs. *The beſt of our Miniſterie* (ſayth *Iames Gibſon* a miniſter of Scotland to a brother in England) *are moſt carefull of your eſtate, and had ſent for that effect, a Preacher of our Church this laſt ſummer (1590.) of purpoſe, to conferre with the beſt affected Miniſters of your Church, to laye downe a plot, how our Church might beſt trauell for your reliefe.* And again: *The Lord knows what care we haue of your Church both in our publike and priuate praiers, &c. For as feeling members of one bodie, we reckon the affliction of your Church to be our owne.*

Gibſon to Ed. Cop.

One *Dauiſon* in like manner (an other miniſter of that countrey) taketh vpon him to iuſtifie the proceedings of our malecontent miniſters here: (as it ſhall herafter more plainely appeare) and for the better incouraging of them in their peeuiſhnes, hee telleth them, *that the iuſt defence of their holie cauſe of Diſcipline muſt not be left, which hath no leſſe warrant to bee continued perpetuallie within the Church, vnder this precept;* Feede my ſheepe: *then hath the preaching of the word and miniſtration of the Sacraments.* Hee doth alſo publiſh it, ſo as the world might take notice of it: *that the good brethren of England, are of the ſame minde with them of Scotland: & that both their cauſes, are moſt neerelie linked together.*

Dauiſon againſt R.B.

Pag, 29.

Pag. 29.
Pag. 20.

Laſtly there is almoſt nothing more ordinary in all the Conſiſtorian diſcourſes and libels of our owne countreymen, whether they bee printed here or in *Scotland*, then to

preſſe

presse vs with the examples of *Geneua* and *Scotland*, and to inueigle the people of *England*, with (I knowe not what) great commendation of the proceedings and platformes of some of the ministers in both those places.

Which points considered, & being required by those that might command me, that whereas certaine writings, and letters were come to my handes, concerning some courses taken by our saide more friendly disturbers, then the Iesuites are, but yet very great disturbers; I should make the same in some sorte knowne: I thought it my best way, for the discharging of my duety therein, first to lay downe before you, the examples, patternes, & proceedings of those Ministers and Churches, which those our factious crew, propound to themselues to follow: & secondly (that I may not bee enforced to passe by them, as * one saith, D. B. was in his sermon at Paules crosse) to make it most apparant vnto you, how artificially and effectually, they haue already by imitation expressed them. Whereby you shall perceiue, that although by reason of their said combination and secretnesse vsed, many things lie hid from those in authority, which they haue done already, in the setting forward of their pretended discipline: yet there will fall out so much to bee disclosed, as laying it to their patternes, you may easily discerne (notwithstanding all their goodly pretences) what to iudge of their proceedings, and whereat in truth they doo ayme.

* Refor. no enemie. B. 2.

Chap. II.

Of the course held at Geneua, *for reformation of religion, & of the doctrine which vpon that occasion hath beene broached.*

IT seemeth, that when the Gospell began first to be preached by *Farellus*, *Viretus*, and others at *Geneua*, they coulde haue beene well content with

with the gouernement of the Bishop there, if hee would willingly haue reiected the Pope, and ioyned with them for the reformation of Religion. This appeareth by M. *Caluins* wordes to Cardinall *Sadolete*. *Talem nobis Hierarchiam si exhibeant, in qua sic emineant Episcopi, vt Christo subesse recusent, vt ab illo tanquam vnico capite pendeant, & ad ipsum referantur; in qua, sic inter se fraternam societatem colant, vt non alio modo, quàm eius veritate, sint colligati: tum vero nullo non anathemate dignos fatear, si qui erunt qui non eam reuerenter summaq; obedientia obseruent. If they doo bring vnto vs such an Hierarchie or priestlie gouernement, wherein the Bishops shall so rule, as that they refuse not to submit themselues to Christ, that they also depend vpon him, as their onely heade, and can be content to referre themselues to him: in which priestlie gouernment they doo so keepe brotherlie societie amongst themselues that they bee knit together by no other knot, then by the trueth: then surelie if there shall be anie, that shall not submit themselues to that Hierarchie or priestlie gouernement, reuerentlie and with the greatest obedience that may be, I confesse there is no kinde of Anathema, or curse, or casting to the diuell; whereof they are not worthie.*

Thus farre then, it must needes be thought, that the Bishoppe was offered by suche as soughte to refourme that Church: which offer he refusing (as I gesse) to accept of, they dealt (as it appeareth by the issue) with the inferiour magistrates and people, to make such a reformation themselues, as they required of them. Whereupon the Bishop beeing Lord of the City, and hauing aswell in his handes, the Soueraigne ciuill Iurisdiction ouer it, or (as *M. Caluin* speaketh) *Ius gladij & alias ciuilis iurisdictionis partes, &c.* as the Ecclesiasticall; they saide, *He was a thiefe and an vsurper*; and so of themselues, with such assistance as was procured, did thrust him from both those authorities. Euen like (in

Cal. to Sadolet.

my

my opinion) as if a Christian Prince, being possessed within his dominions of the supreame Iurisdiction, as well in Ecclesiasticall as in ciuill causes, might vpon the like occasion be serued in the same maner: or, to preuent all exception, as if some Prince of some perticular state or City in *Germanie*, taking vpon him, together with his principality, the calling of a Preacher, Bishop, Superintendent or Ruler of many perticular Churches, (as *George* the Prince *Anhault* did) should in such a case (as the Bishoppe of *Geneua* was) be depriued of both.

Ioach. Camerarius. Phil. Mela. Georg. Maior de vita eius.

The means which was vsed, for such their abandoning of their Bishop, was this. When they perceiued that the Bishop sought, by force to encounter their proceedinges, and that (as *Sleydan* noteth) hee had excited the Duke of *Sauoy*, to that ende, to assist him: they ioyned themselues into a more neere amity with *Berne*. So as the Duke and the Bishop comming together to besiege the City; they were both repulsed, *Bernatibus illis auxilium ferentibus*, *The force of* Berne *assisting the* Geneuians. Since which time (as I suppose) it hath been a principle, with some of the chief Ministers of *Geneua*, (but contrary to the iudgement of all other reformed Churches, for ought I know, which haue not addicted themselues to followe *Geneua*) that *if* Kinges *and Princes refused to refourme Religion, the inferior magistrates or people, by direction of the ministerie, might lawfullie, & ought (if need required) euen by force & armes, to reform it themselues.*

Whittingham in his Preface to Goodmans booke. Knox.

Chap. III.

Of the proceeding of some Scottish Ministers: according to the Geneuian rules of Reformation.

According to the refourming rule, mentioned in the ende of the former Chapter, (to omit some other examples) certaine Ministers in *Scotlande* with their adherents (being meere subiects) haue taken vpon them of later yeares, by a violent and forcible course to reforme Religion.

Knox in his hist. of the church of Scotland, pag. 213

In which course *M. Knox* a man trayned vp at *Geneua*, in the time of *Mary* Queene of England, and very well instructed for such a worke, did shew himselfe to bee a most especiall instrument, as it appeareth by a very strange letter, written by him from *Diepe*, Anno [a] 1557. Wherein hee sheweth, that his opinion and motion of that matter, was not grounded, onely vpon his owne conceit, but vpon the graue counsailes, and iudgement of the most godly and learned, that then liued in *Europe*. (He meaneth the *Geneuians*, *Caluin*, and the rest there.) Vpon this Letter and some other, to and from the sayd K*nox*, *An* [b] *oath of confederacie* was taken amongst his followers, in *Scotland*; and a testification was made of their intents by a kind of subscription.

a Knox pag. 213. ibid.

b Knox p. 217

Immediately after, they prescribed also [c] *Orders* for *Reformation*, to be obserued through all that whole Realme, Anno, 1558. and writ a [d] memorable letter to the *Religious* houses, in the name of the people, that they should either *remoue* thence by such a day, or else *they woulde then eiecte them by force*.

c Knox p. 218

d Knox p. 234

Shortly after (*a Parliament* being there holden by the *Queene Regent*) they [e] *protested* to the same, that except they had their desires, &c. they would proceed in their course: that neither *they nor any that ioined with them, should incurre therefore any danger in life, or landes, or other politicall paines*: and that if *any violence happened in pursuite of those matters, they should thanke themselues*. Afterward, (the *Queene Regent*, seeing all the disorder, that was then, proceeded from such of the ministers) shee [f] *summoned* them to haue appeared at *Striueling*: which they refusing to doo, were therevpon by

e Knox p. 256

f Knox p. 258.

by the *Queenes* commaundement (as it is there tearmed) put to the [g] *Horne*: and all men (vnder paine of rebellion) were inhibited to *aßist* them. But all this notwithstanding, their friends did sticke vnto them. And presently after, vppon a Sermon to that purpose, preached by *M. Knox*, in *Saint* [h] *Iohnstowne*, for the ouerthrowing of Religious houses: they fell the same day to their worke: and within two dayes had quite destroyed and [i] rased in that towne, the houses of the *Blacke Fryars*, of the *Grey Fryars*, and *Charterhouse Moonkes*, downe to the ground. And so they [k] proceeded, breaking downe images and altars, in *Fife*, *Angus*, *Meruis*, and other parts adioyning.

g Knox, pa. 26

h Hollindshed pag. 366. Knox 262

i Knox. p. 263

k Thynne pag. 366. Buchanan.

This course beeing knowne, and therevpon the sayde *Queene* threatning to destroy *Saint Iohnstowne*, they [l] writt vnto her, affirming that *except shee stayed from that crueltie, they should be compelled to take the sword of iust defence*, and *protested*, that, without the Reformation, which they desired, *they would neuer be subiect to anie mortall man*. Then they [m] writte to all their brethren, to repaire vnto them: likewise to *the Nobilitie, vppon paine of* [n] *Excommunication, to ioyne with them*: saying, that it was their duety to *bridle the furie and rage of wicked men, were it of Princes, or Emperours*, *Knox pag. 269*.

l Knox p. 265

m Knox p. 268

n Knox p. 272

Vpon these letters, diuers [o] repaired to *Saint Iohnstowne*, from sundry places: in so much as when *Lyon Herault in his coat armor, commaunded all men, vnder paine of Treason, to returne to their houses, by publike sound of Trumpet, in* Glasco; *neuer a man obeyed that charge, but went forward to their associats*. They [p] writte in like manner to the Bishops and Clergie, that except they desisted from dealing against them, they would *with all force and power, execute iust vengeance and punishment vpon them: and that they would begin that same warre, which God commanded Israell, to execute, against the Cananites*.

o Knox p. 274

p Knox p. 275

q Knox p. 276 This [q] manner of proceeding, they tearmed to be, *the resisting of the enemie.* After (vpon conditions with the *Queene*) this great assembly at *Saint Iohnstowne*, departed thence. But before the seuering of themselues, they entred into a r Knox p. 283 [r] league by *Oath*, that if any one member of their congregation, should be troubled, they should all *concurre, assist, & conuene againe together, for the defence of the same.*

Presently after (vpon a new quarrel against the *Queenes* dealing) an other concourse was made of these reformers, s Knox p. 288 at *Saint* [s] *Androes*: where, by *M Knox* perswasions in his Sermon, they made the like hauocke, that was before at *Saint Iohnstowne*, and did cast downe, spoyle, and destroy, both the houses of the Fryers, and the Abbayes in that towne. So dealt they also within a very short time, with t Knox pag. 298. 299. the Abbay of [t] *Scone*, the *Fryars* at *Strineling*, at *Lithquo*, & Thynne, 367 at *Edenburgh*, the *Queene* [u] being fled thence for feare. u Knox p. 300 *They kept the field* [x] *two moneths*, and tooke away to themselues x Knox p. 306 y Knox p. 308 the [y] *coyning Irons*, (beeing as the Queene alleaged, *a por-* z Knox p. 308 *tion of the patrimonie of the crowne.*) and [z] *iustified the same.* a Knox p. 317. They [a] entred into a League, that though the *Queene sent for them*, they woulde neuer come to her after that time: *without the consent* of their company.

b Knox p. 330 After, the [b] *Queene Regent* made a Proclamation of her desire of peace, and that the state of the Realme, might at c Knox p. 333. the last be at quiet: but they [c] confuted it: & did animate those of their faction (with all their might) to bee alwaies ready, & to stand vpon their guard. They gaue the Queen * Knox p. 362 *the* * *lie* diuers times, and vsed her with most despightfull speeches. And at the length they came to that boldnes, as d Knox p. 364 that they tearmed the *Queenes* part [d] *a faction*: and renouncing their obedience vnto her, protested, that whosoeuer should take her part, *should be punished* as Traytors, *when soeuer God should put the sword of Iustice, into their hands.*

Within

Within a while [e] after, they consulted with their Ministers, especially *M. Wilcocke*, and *M. Knox*, for the deposing of the *Queene Regent*, from her gouernment: who assuring the rest, that *it was lawfull for them so to doo*, processe was made, sentence was giuen, and shee was [f] depriued from all her regiment, by a formall acte, which is set downe in the same storie, penned by *Knox*, and in some part printed after in England.

e Knox p. 372

f Knox p. 378

Not long after this: the *Queene Regent* dyeth. And then they had a *Parliament* by the consent of the french King, and their Queene his wife. In that [g] *Parliament*, held Anno, 1560. they refourmed Religion, and set out a *Confession of the Christian faith*: but *the said King and* [h] *Queene denied, to confirme, or to ratifie the actes thereof, when they were mooued thereunto.* Which thing, (said the confederates, vpon intelligence giuen them) *we little regarded: or yet doo regarde: for all that we did, was rather to shew our duetifull obedience, then to begge of them any strength to our Religion.* And whereas it was obiected, that it coulde not bee a lawfull *Parliament*, where there was neither Scepter, Crowne, nor Sworde borne: they made light of it: [i] saying, that *those were rather, but pompeous and glorious vaine ceremonies, then anie substantiall points, of necessitie required to a lawfull Parliament.* I might proceed much further, in the ripping vp of these and such like practises, for reformation of Religion. But because some peraduenture, will labour to excuse these manner of proceedings, and to colour the same, with some pretence of zeale, and great desire they had, to bee deliuered from Popish Idolatry and Superstition: I haue rather thought it conuenient to let you vnderstande, howe farre they are, from making any such pretences in their owne behalf, and with what new Diuinity-positions, *M. Knox* and *M. Buchanan* haue amplified the *Geneua* resolution (before mentio-

g Knox p. 468

h Knox p. 500

i Knox p. 502

 ned,)

ned,) to the iustification not only of all their said attempts and actions, but of many other of the like nature, which (since those times) haue beene there also practised.

Chap. IIII.

How the Geneuian Doctrine, or principle for Reformation, hath beene amplified, by certaine pretended Reformers in Scotland.

k Knox p.216 Knox appel. fol.28. l Knox app.25 m Knox to the Comminalty f.49.50

Eformation [k] *of Religion, doth belonge to more, then the Clergie and the King.*

Noble men [l] *ought to reforme Religion, if the King will not.*

Reformation [m] *of Religion, belongeth to the Comminaltie.*

n ibid. fol.47 *The Comminaltie,* [n] *concurring with the Nobilitie, may compell the Bishops to cease from their tirrannie.*

o ibid. fol.55 *The* [o] *Comminaltie by their power, may bridle the cruell beasts (the Priests.)*

p ibid. fol.55 *The* [p] *Comminaltie, may lawfullie require of their King, to haue true Preachers: and if he be negligent, they iustlie may themselues prouide them, maintaine them, defende them, against all that doo persecute them, and may detaine the profits of the Church liuings, from the other sort.*

q Knox histo. pag.343. *God hath* [q] *appointed the Nobilitie, to bridle the inordinate appetites of Princes, and in so doing, they cannot be accused, as resisters of authoritie.*

r Knox appel, fol.33. *It is their* [r] *dutie, to represse the rage and insolencie of Princes.*

s Knox appel. fo.28.30, &c. *The* [s] *Nobilitie and Comminaltie, ought to reforme Religion, and in that case, may remoue from honours, and may punish such, as God hath cōdemned, Deu.12.* (he meaneth Idolaters, &c.) *of what estate, condition, or honour soeuer.*

t Knox appel. fol.30 *The* [t] *punishment of such crimes, as touch the Maiestie of God, doth not appertaine to Kinges and chiefe rulers onelie, but also to the*

the whole bodie of the people, and to euerie member of the same, as occasion, vocation, and abilitie shall serue, to reuenge the iniurie done against God.

The people [u] *are bound by oath to God, to reuenge (to the vtmost of their power) the iniurie, done against his Maiestie,*

u Knox appel. fol. 35.

The cruell murthering of the *Archbishoppe of Saint Androwes*, in his bed-chamber, 1545: by three priuate gentlemen, because (as they told him,) he had beene, and so remained an obstinate enemie to the Gospel, is sought to be iustified lately in print, to bee a godly acte: & incouragement is giuen for others, in the like case to commit the like outrage.

Historie of the Church of Scotl. pa. 187.

Princes, for * *iust causes may be deposed.*

* Knox histor. Pag. 372.

It is not [a] *birthright onely, nor propinquity of bloud, that maketh a King, lawfullie to raigne aboue a people, professing Christ Iesus.*

a knox to England and Scot. fol. 77.

If Princes [b] *be tyrants, against God and his truth, their subiects are freed from their oaths of obedience.*

b knox ibid. folio 78.

Populus rege [c] est præstantior & melior: *the people are better then the King, and of greater authoritie.*

c Buch. de iure regni page. 61.

Populo [d] ius est, vt imperium cui velit deferat: *the people haue right, to bestow the Crowne at their pleasure.*

d Ibid pa. 13.

Penes [e] populum est, vt leges ferat: sunt reges veluti tabulariorum custodes. *The making of lawes, doth belong to the people: and Kings are but as the Masters of the Rolles.*

e ibid pag. 25

The people, [f] *haue the same power, ouer the King: that the King hath ouer any one person.*

f ibid pag. 58.

It were [g] *good, that rewardes were appointed by the people, for such as should kill tyrants: as commonly there is, for those,* qui lupos aut vrsos occiderunt, aut catulos eorum deprehenderunt: *that haue killed either wolues or beares, or taken their whelpes.*

g ibid pag. 40.

The [h] *people may arraigne their Prince.*

h ibid pag 61.

The

ibid pag. 70 *The*[i] *Ministers may excommunicate him.*

k ibid pag. 70 *He, that*[k] *by excommunication, is cast into hell; is not worthy to enioy any life vpon earth.*

And wheras there are sufficient, and sound obiections, made, by such as haue truely reprooued these dangerous assertions: Behold I pray you, their answers, worthy to be known and remembred, to the euerlasting discredit of the authors, framers, and partakers with them.

Chap. V.

The obiections against the doctrine, reported of in the former chapter, with the Consistorian answers vnto them.

Buc. de iur. regni. pag. 49. *Obiection.* Custome, [l] is against such dealing with Princes.

Answere. *There is nothing more daungerous to bee followed* (publica via) *then custome.*

m Knox appe. fol. 26. *Ob.* We must [m] obey Kings, be they good or bad.

Ans. *It is blasphemie to say so.*

n Buch. de iure regni. pag. 53. *Ob.* Ieremie [n] commaunded obedience to Nabuchodonozer.

Ans. *The example is but singular.*

o Ibid. pag. 57 *Ob.* God placeth [o] tyrants sometimes for the punishment of his people.

Ans. *So doth he priuate men sometimes to kill them.*

p ibid. pag. 57 *Ob.* The [p] Iewes dealt not so with their Kings.

Ans. *Their Kinges were not first elected by the people; and therefore they might not: but ours haue nothing but from the people.*

q ibid. pag. 57 *Ob.* Shew an [q] example out of the Scriptures, that subiects may vse their gouernours in this sort.

Ans. *The argument is not good: it cannot bee shewed in the Scriptures, therefore it is vnlawfull.* Possum apud multas nationes,

tiones, plurimas & saluberrimas recensere leges, quarum in sacris litteris nullum est exemplum. *I can shewe sundrie good and wholesome lawes, in diuers countries, of the which lawes there is no example in the Scriptures.*

Ob. Saint Paul[r] doth commaund vs to pray for Princes. *1. Tim. 2.* r ibid pag. 50

Ans. *Wee may punish theeues, and yet wee ought to pray for them.*

Ob. Saint Paule[s] doth command vs to be subiect and obedient to Princes. *Tit. 3.* s ibid p. 50. 55

Ans. *Paule writt this in the infancie of the Church. There were but fewe Christians then, and not many of them rich, or of abilitie, so as they were not ripe for such a purpose.*

As if[t] a man should write to such Christians as are vnder the Turke, in substance poore, in courage feeble, in strength vnarmed, in number fewe, and generallie subiect to all kinde of iniuries: would he not write as Paul did? So as the Apostle, did respect the men he writt vnto: and his wordes are not to be extended, to the body or people of a common wealth, or whole Citie. t Ibid. pag. 56 Note this Diuinity

For imagine (sayth[u] hee) *that Paul were now aliue, where both the King and people do professe Christianity, and that there were such Kings, as would haue their becks to stand for lawes: as cared neither for God nor man: as bestowed the Church reuenues* scurris & balatronibus *vpon iesters and rascalls, and such as gibed at those that did embrace the more sincere Religion: what would he write of such to the Church? Surely except he would dissent from himself, he would say, that he accounted no such for Magistrates: hee would forbidde all men for speaking vnto them, and from keeping them companie: he would leaue them to their subiects to be punished: neither would he blame them, if they accounted no longer such for their Kings, as by the law of God, they could haue no societie withall.* And thus farre the answearer. u ibi, p. 56. 57

There are diuers other obiections against those reformers:

mers: which receiue almost as desperate answers. But I will not at this time trouble you with them, especially if you will giue me leaue to aduertise you, that this new Diuinity of dealing thus with Princes, is not onely helde by *Knox* and *Buchanan*, but generally (for ought I can learne) by most of the Consistorians of chiefe name beyonde the Seas, who (being of the *Geneua* humor) doo endeuour by most vniust & disloyall meanes, to subiect to their forged presbyteries, the scepters and swordes of Kings and Princes: as *Caluin*, *Beza*, *Hotoman*, *Vrsinus*, (as he commeth out from *Newstadt*) *Vindiciæ contra tyrannos*, *Eusebius Philadelphus*, *&c.* For the further fruit of which Consistorian Diuinitie, (besides that which is sayd by some of the Ministers of *Scotland*) I referre you to the consideration of such stirres, as haue hapned of late yeares, in some other countries. And thus farre concerning the iustification, which is made of the Scottish reformation. Now I will leade you backe againe, where I left: vz. to certaine of the Ministers further proceedings there; vppon these aforesaide maine grounds and principles.

Chap. VI.

The proceedinges of certaine Scottish Ministers, according to the grounds mentioned in the two last chapters, for setting vp of the Consistorian Discipline, and of their vrging of our English Disciplinaries, to follow their steppes.

t Knox hist. pag. 502.

THe Parliament [t] of Scotland before mentioned Chap 3. of An. 1560. being dissolued, there was then *a booke of Discipline*, or newe kingdome of Christ (by their seuerall presbyteries) drawne and compiled after the *Geneua* fashion, by *M. Knox* and others. Which booke, vpon the offering of it to their associates and fauo-

rites,

rites,to be allowed,receiued,and publikely practiſed,was by them reiected,and tearmed to bee in truth,but *a deuout imagination.* Whereupon now riſeth,an occaſion of a new hiſtorie,how (after they had obtained reformation of religion, as touching the true preaching of the worde, and adminiſtration of the Sacraments)they alſo dealt and preuailed in the ende, for the eſtabliſhing of their Diſcipline and Conſiſtoriall gouernement.

It [u] *appeareth*, that in the foreſaide ſpoyles of Abbayes, Fryeries,and Cathedrall Churches,&c.euery man almoſt did ſeeke his priuate commoditie. Which beeing eſpied before by the ſaide Miniſters, they miſliked it: (as finding the pray taken out of their teeth:) but yet they were gone ſo far belike,as that there was no remedie. They told them of it in their ſermons in ſome ſort then,as it ſhould appear. Marry nowe, when they came to the ende of their trauaile,the hope of their glory,the erecting of their gouernment, and their raigne ouer all, and doo finde themſelues croſſed therein: blame them not, though they were not a little angry. Then * they gaue it out againſt their owne fauourers afore, *that ſome were licentious:* ſome *had greedilie griped the poſſeſsions of the Church:* others *thought they would not lacke their part of Chriſts coate*, yea, *and that before that euer he was hanged.*

u Knox hiſt. pag.468.

* Knox hiſt, pag.503.

Of a Noble man,that refuſed to ſubſcribe to their Diſcipline,(as they call it) they writ thus. *He had a very euill woman to his wiſe: if the poore, the ſchooles, and the miniſterie of the Church had their owne, his Kitchen would lacke two parts and more of that,which he vniuſtlie now poſſeſſeth.* And generally to the like effect: *there were none within this Realme, more vnmercifull to the poore Miniſters, then were they, which had greateſt rents of the Church. But in that we haue perceiued the old prouerbe to be true: nothing can ſuffice a wretch.* And a-

Ibidem.

y In the conclusion of their booke of Discipline.

gaine, *the bellie, hath no eares*. They [y] threatned the greatest men of the lande, with Gods heauy punishments, if they should reiect that Discipline, ascribing it to their *blind affection*, to their *respect of carnal friends*, to their *corrupt iudgement*, and to their *former iniquities*, and *present ingratitude*. But [a] (notwithstanding, that some refused to subscribe to this booke, which made the Ministers so angry:) yet by sundry cunning deuises, raylings, threatnings, &c. many yeelded thereunto, and did promise, thereby *to set the same forward, to the vttermost of their powers.*

a Knox histo. pag. 504.

This subscription thus in sort obtained, they began to put the same in practise. They [b] *appointed to haue their assemblies both particular and generall.* They [c] exercised iurisdictions, and *appointed one* Saunderson *to be carted for adulterie:* but he was rescued. A great [d] vprore arising *in Edenburgh, about the making of a Robinhood, they of the Consistorie did excommunicate the whole multitude.* The *Bishops* [e] seeking to encounter and represse them in their practises, they professed that they would not *suffer their pride and Idolatrie*. They [f] caused diuers places (as they tearmed them) of superstition, to be burnt: I thinke they meane some *Bishops* houses) as [g] *Palsay*, the *Bishop* also narrowly escaping them.

b Declaration B. 1. 2.
c Knox histo. pag. 523.
d ibid. pa. 527
e ibid. pa. 531.
f ibid. pa. 334
g Knox Iust. 534.

The *Bishops* hauing embraced the Gospel, it was at first agreed euen by the brethren, with the consent of the *Regent*, that *the Bishops estate should be* * *maintained and authorised.* This endured for sundry yeares: but then there was no remedie, the calling it selfe of *Bishops* was at last become *Antichristian*, and downe they must of necessitie. Whervpon [h] *they commanded the Bishops (by their owne authoritie) to leaue their Offices and their Iurisdictions.*

* Declaration B. 2.
h ibid B. 2.

They [i] decreed in their assemblies, that *Bishops shoulde haue no voices in Parliament*: and that done, they desired of the King, that such Commissioners (as they should sende

i ibid. B. 2.

to the Parliament and Councell) might from thence forth be authorized in the *Bishops* places, for the estate. They *also directed their Commissioners to the Kings Maiestie* : commanding him and the Councell, *vnder paine of the censures of the Church* (meaning excommunication) *to appoint no Bishops in time to come, because they* (the brethren) *had concluded, that state to be vnlawfull.*

Hereof as it seemeth they writt to *Geneua* , their newe *Rome*, or *Metropolitane* Citty . From whence they were greatly animated, and earnestly perswaded, to continue in that course. *Beza* [k] the Consistorian *Patriarche*, assureth them that they had done well, and mooueth them, *ne vnquam illam pestem admittant, quamuis vnitatis retinendæ specie blandiatur: that they would neuer admit againe that plague,* (meaning the calling of *Bishoppes*) *although it might allure them, with colour of keeping vnitie.* k Epistola 79.

After they had discharged the *Bishops*, (as it hath beene noted) they agreed amongst themselues, to haue *their* [l] *Superintendents*. But that deuise continued not long: for in the ende it was determined , that needes all Ministers of the word, must be equall. And then (especially) their Presbyteries began to flourish. They tooke vpon [m] them (with their adherents) *to vsurpe the whole Ecclesiasticall Iurisdiction.* They *altered the lawes after their owne appetite*. They *assembled* [n] *the Kings subiects, and enioyned Ecclesiasticall paines vnto them.* They *made Decrees, and put the same in execution.* They *vsed* [o] *very trayterous, seditious, and contumelious words, in the pulpits, schooles, and otherwise, to the disdaine and reproch of the King, and being called to answere the same, they vtterlie disclaimed the Kings authoritie*: saying, *he* [p] *was an incompetent Iudge, and that matters of the Pulpit ought to be exempted from the iudgement & correction of Princes.* They [q] *prescribed lawes to the King and State.* They *appointed* [r] *Fasts throughout*

l Declaration B.3.

m Declaration B.1.

n Act of Parliament ca.4.

o Ibid. cap.2.

p Decl.A.3.

q Decl.B.3.

r Decl.B.3.

the whole Realme, especially when some of their faction were to mooue any great enterprise.

With these manner of proceedings, the King there, and the State, finding great cause of iust discontentment and danger: after diuers consultations and good deliberation, order was taken about the yeare, 1582. for the checking & redressing of them. His Maiesty began to take vpon him his lawfull authoritie, belonging to all Christian Princes, in causes Ecclesiasticall. Wherupon he caused the foresaid courses, held by the Ministers, to be examined and looked into. And they were found to be such, as that *some of them were remoued from their charges, some were imprisoned, & some indighted. Commaundement was also giuen, that they should not proceede, in the execution of their Ecclesiasticall censures, as they had done. A Proclamation was made in diuers of the chiefest places in the Realme, for discharging the Ministers of their foresaid conuentions and assemblies, vnder paine, to bee punished as Rebels.* They were published in that Proclamation, to be *vnnaturall subiects, seditious persons, troublesome and vnquiet spirites, members of Sathan, enemies to the King, and the Common-wealth of their natiue countrey:* and were *charged to desist from preaching, in such sort as they did,* amongst other matters against the authoritie in Church causes, against the calling of Bishops, & for the maintenance of their former proceedings.

Declaration 1582.

But the issue of the Kinges good intention to haue refourmed these disorders, was this: In August 1582. his Highnesse being drawn vnto a certain Noble mans house to be feasted in Rutheuen: there *he was surprised & restrained.* Which attempt was qualified and tearmed (in *a Declaration set out,* 1582. to iustifie the same) *to be onely a repaire of the Kings faithfull subiects, to his Highnes presence, and to remaine with him, for resisting of the present dangers appearing to*

Act of Parliament, 1584. cap. 7.

Declara. 1582

Gods

Gods true religion,&c. and for the remouing from his Maiestie, the chiefe authors thereof.

After a time, the King deliuered himselfe out of their hands, that so had restrained him: and by the aduise of his three estates assembled in Councell, (notwithstanding the saide qualification or pretence of repayre) the action in it self *was iudged and published in December, 1583. to be* Crimen lesæ Maiestatis, *the Offence of Treason*: and some were executed for it, others fled, and diuers of the Ministers, that had bin dealers in that matter, pretending they were persecuted, escaped into *England*. Act of Parl. 1584. cap. 7.

With this his Maiesties course for Reformation, the Disciplinarian faction was greatly displeased: and did proceede in their Consistorian humour accordingly. In an assembly of Ministers and Elders (forsooth) at *Edenburgh*, shortly after, the State of the Realme was stoutly encountred. For although the King, with the aduise of his estates, had resolued the saide fact of surprising his Maiesties person, to be treasonable, *yet the brethren did not onely authorise and avow the same, but also, esteeming their owne iudgements, to be the soueraigne iudgement of the Realme, did ordaine all them to be excommunicated, that would not subscribe vnto that their iudgement.* Declar. 1585.

About the same time, or not long after, vz. in Aprill, 1583. *there was another most treasonable conspiracie and rebellion attempted at* Sterling, *and intended to haue beene further executed and prosecuted against his Highnesse person:* and all vnder pretence of Religion, and chiefly (in shewe) for the Consistorian or Presbyteriall soueraignetie. Act of Parl. 1584. cap. 7.

With these and many more such vnduetifull insolencies, the King and State there, beeing greatly mooued: a Parliament was called, and held in May, 1584. wherein order was taken, for a generall Reformation in causes Ecclesiasticall, throughout the whole Church of *Scotland*.

u Act of Parl. cap.2. The Kings [u] lawfull authority in causes Ecclesiasticall, so often before impugned, was approued and confirmed; and it was *made treason*, for any man to refuse to answere before the King, though it were concerning any matter, which was Ecclesiasticall.

* ibid, cap.20 The third * estate of Parliament, (that is, *the Bishoppes*) *was restored to the auncient dignity:* it was [y] made *treason*, for

y ibid, cap.3. any man after that time to procure the *innouation or diminution* of the power and authority of any of the three estates.

z ibid cap. 4. The foresayd [z] iudgements, Senates, and Presbyteriall iurisdictions were discharged: and it was enacted in these words: *that after that time none should presume, or take vppon them to conuocate, conuene, or assemble themselues together, for holding of Councells, conuentions, or assemblies, to treat, consult, or determine in any matter of estate, ciuill or Ecclesiasticall, (excepting the ordinary iudgements:) without the Kinges especiall commandement.*

a ibid cap.7. It was [a] further then ordayned, *that none of his Highnesse subiects, in time comming, should presume to take vppon them by worde or writing, to iustifie the most treasonable attempt at* Ruthuen, *or to keepe in Register or store, any bookes approouing the same in any sort.*

b ibid, cap. 8. An Acte [b] was also made, for the calling in of *Buchanans Chronicle*, and his booke *de iure regni apud Scotos.*

c ibid.cap.8. Lastly (sayth the *Acte* [c] *of Parliament* it selfe.) *Forasmuch as through the wicked, licentious, publike, and priuate speeches, and vntrue calumnies of diuers his Highnesse subiects, to the disdaine, contempt, and reproach of his Maiestie, his Councell, and proceedinges, stirring vp his Highnesse subiectes thereby, to misliking, sedition, vnquietnes, to cast off their due obedience to his Maiestie. Therefore it is ordained, that none of his subiects*

shall

shall presume, or take vpon them, priuatelie or publikelie, in sermons, declamations, or familiar conferences, to vtter any false, slanderous, or vntrue speeches, to the disdaine, reproach, and contempt of his Maiestie, his Councell, and proceedings, or to meddle in the affaires of his Highnesse vnder paine, &c.

And thus you haue seene some part of the practise of the *Geneua* resolution in *Scotland*, for their booke of *Discipline*; and reformation in Religion. But yet I must needes draw you on a little further.

Presently, after that the sayde Parliament was ended, notwithstanding the kings maiesty, had in the same [d] most royally & religiously cōfirmed with great sincerity the articles of true Religion, for preaching the worde, and administration of the sacraments accordingly, and had likewise vnited to his Crowne, the supreame authority in all causes within his Realme, aswell Ecclesiasticall as Ciuill: yet (because their Presbyterial soueraignty was therby abridged) diuers very spitefull, disloyall, and slaunderous speeches were cast abroade, by them and their associates, against his Highnesse.

d cap. 1. of that Parliament, &c.

For they [e] gaue out, as though the King *had beene declined to Popery, and had made Acts to derogate the free passage of the Gospell*: that *he endeuored* [f] *to extinguish the light of the Gospell*: that there was *left nothing of the whole auncient forme of iustice and pollicie in the spirituall state, but a naked shadow*, with many other the like reprochfull and calumnious reportes, which they spread abroad in their owne Country.

e Declar. A. 2.

f Thinnes addition to Hollinshed. pa. 446. D. A.

Diuers of [g] the chiefe Ministers of that faction likewise that were fled out of *Scotland* into *England*, for feare of punishment, in respect of many their great and haynous offences, pretended (as it hath beene noted) that they fledd hether, because they were persecuted at home for their consciences, and could not be suffered to preach the Gos-

g Archbishop of Saint. Androwes Letter, and of other *Preachers*.

M. Hutchinsons Letter and as he is readie to be deposed.

pell. One [h] *Dauison* (a *Scottish* Minister) so rayled against the King of Scots in the pulpit, at the parish Church of the olde Iury in London, that vpon complaint made thereof, by the Lord Ambassador of *Scotland*, direction was giuen to the Lord Bishop of London, for the silencing of all the *Scottish* Ministers in the City.

i *Thinnes* addition. page. 446.

And this disloyall and slaunderous course was helde, both in *Scotland* and *England*, so farre as they [i] durst, from May, vntill Nouember following.

k ibid Thinn.

l The *Procla*mation is there also set downe.

At what time, this stratagem here ensuing was wroght (as I am perswaded) by the Consistorians instigation. The King [k] of *Scotland*, being vpon occasion of *a contract*, nere *Strirueling*: heard of certaine enemies (*as hee then accounted them*) comming towards him. Whereupon his Maiesty *raysing such power as hee could, conuayed himselfe to* Strirueling. Where before he looked for them, ten thousand men *presented themselues* in armes. *They pitched their Tents before the towne the first of Nouember*, and there made a Proclamation in their owne names, commanding all the Kings subiects to assist them. Many pretenses [l] are alleaged of that their attempt. And these namely: that whereas there had beene *Acts and Proclamations* a little before *published against the Ministerie and Clergie, inhibiting their Presbyteries, assemblies and other exercises, priuileges, and immunities*: and that *the most learned and honest were compelled, for safetie of their liues and consciences, to abandon their Country, &c.* Nowe the *afflicted Church might be comforted, and all the said Acts lately made in preiudice of the same, might bee solemnely cancelled, and for euer adnulled.* This Proclamation thus knowne, the King fortified the towne as he could: but to no purpose. For within two houres assault it was wonne. The King thereupon, was enforced to flye *vnto the Castle.* The Conquerours of the towne, *placed their ensignes before the blockehouse of the Castle*,

Castle, and so ordred the matter, that there was no way for any in the Castle to escape their hands.

Wherupon (a parley being concluded) the King desired by his Commissioners three petitions: The first, *That his life, honor, and estate might be preserued.* The second, *That the liues of certain of his friends with him might not be touched.* The third, *That all things might be transacted peaceably.* The other side, by their Commissioners likewise desired other three petitions: The first, *That the King would allow of their intention, and subscribe their Proclamation, vntill further order were established by the estates, &c.* and *that he would deliuer vnto them, all the strong Holds in the land.* The second, *That the disquieters of the Common-wealth might be deliuered vnto them and abide their due tryall by Law.* The third, *That the old guard might be remooued, and another placed.*

Vppon mutuall relation from the Commissioners on both sides, the parties that were assembled in armes, did yeeld vnto the first and third of the Kings petitions: and the King graunting to all theirs, as there was no remedy, committed himselfe into their hands, and had a new guard immediately appointed to attend him.

And thus the Presbyteries of *Scotland* by the Kings subscribing to the foresaid Proclamation, recouered againe a great part of their strength. But not all (as it seemeth) vpon the sodaine: which was the occasion of a new stirre. For presently after the sayde Noble victory, the *Scottish* Ministers that were in England, (hauing al their former disloyalties vppon composition remitted;) made their repayre without delay into *Scotland*: where finding not such readinesse as they expected, for a more authenticall repealing of the statutes made in the foresaid Parliament, 1584. they began (notwithstanding the Kings late goodnes towards them,) to exclaime in their Pulpits, with most proud and bitter

This appeareth by James Gibsons conference with the King, penned by himselfe, and deliuered abroad in many Copies.

bitter Inuectiues against him.

One *Iames Gibson*, compared his Maiesty publikely in his preachings, *vnto Ieroboam*, tearmed *him a persecutor*, and *threatned him*, that if he tooke that course, he should be the *last of his race.*

Gibson hath penned this matter as Cōsistorianly, as Catiline himselfe could haue done it.

And being called for such his disloyall *speeches*, before the King & Councell, the xxj. of December, 1585. he very boldly iustified the same: saying to his Highnesse, *As long as you maintayne these cursed Actes of 1584. the tyranny of Bishops, &c. Ye are a Persecutor.* And againe, *As Ieroboam for the leading of the people of Israell from the lawes of the house of Iudah, and from the true worshipping of God, to serue Idolatry, was rooted out, he and all his posterity: so should the King) if he continued in that cursed course, maintaining those wicked Acts against God) be rooted out, and conclude that race, &c.*

What else hath fallen out since that time, by reason of the raines, which now (as it hath beene noted) these zealous brethren haue gotten to themselues, and how moderately and duetifully they doo proceede, in the practise of their Presbyteries, and Consistorian Kingdomes: the articles, which the King not long since offred vnto the Ministers, to haue beene subscribed vnto by them, doo sufficiently declare and make manifest. *Ex malis moribus nascuntur bonæ leges: Out of ill maners spring good and wholsome lawes.*

The coppie of these articles, was deliuered abroad by some of her Maiesties priuie Counsell.

The chiefe and especiall pointes of the sayde articles are these: that *all Preachers there, should yeelde their obedience to the Kings Maiesty:* that *they should not pretend any Priuiledge in their allegeance*: that *they should not meddle in matters of State:* that *they should not publikely reuile his Maiesty*: that *they should not draw the people from their due obedience to the King: & that when they are accused, vpon their facts or speeches, or for refusing to doo things, &c.* they *should not alledge the inspiration of the holy spirit, nor serue themselues with colour of conscience, but confesse*

fesse their offences as men, and to craue pardon as subiects, &c.

It is great pitty, that so worthy a Christian King, should be driuen to require such a subscription in his owne kingdome, especially of those men, that should be lights to the rest, and the chiefe examples of all ductifull obedience: It is more to be pittied, that (for ought I can learne) his Maiesty cannot as yet obtaine so much at their handes. But most of all it is to be lamented, that no man can gesse (for ought I know) how far this Gangrene will spread it selfe.

At the first, they found but faults against the *Bishops*, but after they ouerthrewe them. The *Anabaptists in Germany began with the Bishops and Clergy, but they ended with the ciuill Magistrate.* Consider of *Buchanans* dealing, whether he maketh not the like assault against Princes, that his companions did against *Bishops*; as in deriding their titles, misliking their pompe, and in glancing at their reuenues. He tearmeth [a] the honorable phrases of *Maiesty, Highnesse, and Lordship*, solæcismos & barbarismos aulicos, *that is, vnlawfull & corrupt kinds of speech, which are vsed in Court, and doo proceede* (as he sayth) *from flattery*. Hee gibeth [b] at the state which Princes take vpon them, when they shewe themselues to the people, comparing *them to Childrens puppets, which are garishly attyred.*

Bullinger.

a Epistle to the king of Scots before his booke de iure regni &c

b De iure regni pa. 17.

After [c] also, he insinuateth that a good Prince *should appeare & come abroad, only defended with his innocencie*, non superbo spiculatorum & μαχαιροφόρων cætu, sericatisq; nebulonibus stipatus: *not with a proud company of guarders, and of pensioners, and of silken knaues.* He would haue Kings to content themselues with lesse *reuenues and seruice, commending the Discipline of Laconia, where it was strange to haue one man pull off an other mans sockes, at his going to bedde:* and likewise the example of *Pelagius*, that first discomfited the Saracens in *Spaine*: in that *he had his house*, not built after the fashion

c Ibid. pa. 34.

now a dayes, with many stately roomes of honor, but was contented *with one place for himselfe, his fire, his friends, and his cattell*, (after the Irish fashion.)

But to let passe these contempts and pointes of *Anabaptisme*: one thing more is likewise to be considered in these *Scottish* reforming ministers, which they haue sucked from their *Mother-City Geneua*. They cannot be content, to haue raysed vp sedition and troubles at home, to haue slandred both far and nere, the most Godly reformation of Religion, which their King had made there, and to erect (you haue seene how) in place thereof a meere counterfeit plot of a new *Popish* tyranny, such a one as hath already quite ouerthrown the auncient estate of that Church, & wroght more mischiefe in that Country in thirty yeares, then the Pope of *Rome* had done before (as I thinke) in fiue hundred: But they presume also, much further then becommeth them, to cast some of their contentious and disloyall seedes into *England*.

Melancton. *Vulpecula* (cauda amissa) reliquis vulpibus callidè persuasit vt similiter & ipsæ caudas resecarent, ne sola turpis & deformis in suo genere videretur. The Fox (hauing lost her tayle) craftely persuaded the other Foxes, that they would likewise cut off their tayles, least she herselfe alone, should seeme the foule and deformed beast of all that kinde*. And hence it commeth (as I take it) that to bring the flourishing estate of our Church in *England* into the same misery, that theirs is brought into, they rayle, deuise, and clap their handes, to set vs here together by the eares.

e Dauison in the name of the rest, in a booke of his lately published. Page. 2.
f pag. 29.

Some of them say, that [e] *our Church is still vnder the bondage of an Antichristian gouernement*: that *our Bishops are a hurtfull relique of Romish confusion*: that [f] *they thrust with side and shoulder to make hauocke of the Church, by a disguised persecution*, and *that they do tyrannize aboue their brethren with violence*

olence[g] *and crueltie.* g pag. 28.

They vse these words of her excellent Maiesty. *Alacke good*[h] *Princesse, the true report of thinges commeth seldome to her eares.* And do very grossely insinuate, nay indeed plainly affirme, that *there are in Court some crafty*[i] *miscreants, which doo abuse her Maiesty,* whom *they resemble to Ioab, Iesabell, Haman and Gehasi.* h pag. 28. i pag. 12.

They doo[k] *iustifie the proceedings of our disturbers here,* & *animating*[l] *them to go forward* as they haue begun, doo tell them, *that both their causes* (vz. their owne in *Scotland*, and of our factions in *England*) *are most nerely*[m] *linked together:* and *doo*[n] *promise, that they will not cease to commend their troubled state vnto God, in their priuate and publike prayers.* They[o] compare our hindring in *England* of the pretended Discipline, vnto *the hinderance, which Gods enemies made, vnto the building of Ierusalem.* They seeke vnder hand[p] to steale away the harts of her Maiesties subiects, especially of those that haue beene, and still are seduced, by our Consistorian Schismatikes: by putting them in hope of *one Darius, that after a time shall giue full authority for the sayde building of Ierusalem.* Which manner of dealing, there is no *Darius* liuing, could take in good part, if the like practises were vsed by others amongst his people. k pag. 3. l pag. 21. m pag. 20. n pag. 29. o pag. 20. p pag. 21.

GOD of his infinite mercy, graunt vnto her Maiesty, a long, a prosperous, and a happy raigne ouer vs: and so knit the harts of all true English men, vnto their Queene of Saba, their *Hester*, and their most royall *Elizabeth*, that without the expectation of any *Darius* whosoeuer, they may euer continue her most loyall, faithfull, and obedient subiects, rather wishing in their soules, that the world with her Maiesty should end their dayes together, then once to take ioy, by the least imagination of any future change. Amen.

And thus much of the manner and wayes vsed by certaine Scottish Ministers, for Reformation and Discipline. Which pointes or Consistorian proceedinges, I haue not touched (as God knoweth) with any minde or intent, to dishonour the state of that Country. Besides, much may well be sayd (I assure my selfe) in excuse of such of the laity; as ioyned in the premisses. For I finde they were led with a very great zeale. They had beene so long imprisoned in the darkenesse of Popery, that when the Gospell appeared vnto them, it so dazeled their eyes, as that for very gladnesse they considered not well, what they did, so they might enioy it. Their goods, their lands, their wiues and their children, nay their liues (in respect therof) were not greatly deare vnto them.

Moreouer it is manifest, how long they were exercised with great feare and many perplexities, what entertainement and continuance the Gospell should finde amongst them. In which case euery man may easily coniecture, how easie a matter it was for them, to be miscaried by their teachers & Preachers: perswading them, that by Gods commandement they were bound to vndertake that course, & withall not omitting great threates of excommunication & damnation, if they refused so to doo. They found their sayd Ministers doctrine very good and sound, in the chiefe points of saluation: and who would then haue suspected them in matters of lesse importance?

So as whatsoeuer was done amisse by them, as touching their proceedings mentioned, I doo (wholly in a manner) ascribe it to their Ministers of the *Geneua* learning. Vnto whom also it ought of right to be imputed, that I or any other, either haue, or hereafter shall haue, any occasion at all so much as once to make mention of the least thing, that might be any waies offensiue to the meanest of that natiō.

For

For what had I, or any other priuate man in England, to doo with their matters, otherwise then to haue prayed for them: had their sayd Ministers, but onely taken vppon them to haue iustified their sayde proceedinges, by their owne Lawes, customes, and priuiledges, and could haue contented themselues to haue gone no further? Marry nowe that the chiefest of them, for the excusing of themselues, and that they might shew, whose schollers they are, haue presumed to publish (and that in print) such strange & seditious doctrine, as doth tend to the like disturbance, and indeede to the vtter ouerthrow of the freest and most absolute Monarchies, that are or can be in Christendome, not omitting withall, to solicite and incourage our pretended reformers in England, to proceed as they haue begun, in following their steps, contrary (I am sure) both to the word of God, and to all the lawes and customes of this Realme: I am in very good hope, that there is no man of any sound iudgement, who will be offended with mee, in that to disclose, and thereby to preuent such mischiefes, as might otherwise ensue with vs, I haue beene bolde to lay downe (but yet out of their printed bookes) some of the proceedinges of the sayde Ministers of *Scotland*, which at this time our owne Preachers in England, of the Disciplinarian consort, (as nowe it followeth to bee shewed) doo take vppon them to imitate, and haue already proceeded further in them, then some of their fauorers will acknowledge or (I thinke) doo as yet suspect.

Buchanan. The historie of the church of Scotland. Knox.

The end of the first Booke.

*F THE

THE SECOND BOOKE OF DISCIPLINARY GROVNDES and Practises.

Chap. I.

The doctrine of certaine English Ministers, which they learned at Geneua, *and published of purpose to haue procured the like course for reformation in England, to that which was in Scotland.*

AS you haue hearde in the first Booke, howe *M. Knox* beeing at *Geneua* in *Q. Maries* time, laboured and afterward proceeded to reforme Religion in *Scotland* by force and armes: so did sundry *English* men, that then liued there in like sort, according to the *Geneua* resolution in that point, endeuour as much as lay in them, to haue kindled the like stirres at that time here in *England*. To which especiall ende, they did write hither sundry letters and bookes, wholy of this argument: vz. *that the then Councellors; the Noble men; inferiour Magistrates; and (rather then faile) the very people; were bound before God to ouerthrowe the superstition and Idolatrie that was then in the Land, and to reforme Religion, whether the Queene would or no: yea though it were by putting her to death:* Out of two of these *English* bookes, I haue collected these seditious and consistoriall propositions following.

All

All men, councellors, noble men, inferior magistrates, and people are bound and charged, to see the lawes of God kept, and to suppresse and resist Idolatrie, by force. Goodman. Page 73. ibid. pag. 74. ibid. pag. 77.

If the magistrates shall refuse, to put massemongers and false preachers to death, the people (in seeing it performed) doo shewe that zeale of God, which was commended in Phinees, *destroying the adulterers, and in the* Israelites *against the* Beniamites. ibid. pag. 196

To teach, that it was not lawfull in any case to resist the superior powers, but rather to submit our selues to punishment is a dangerous doctrine, taught by some, by the permission of God for our sinnes. ibid. page 30.

It is not sufficient for subiects, not to obey wicked commandements of their Princes, but to withstand them also, in dooing the contrarie, euerie man in his vocation and office. ibid. page 63. 43. 59. 72.

Shieriffes, Iaylors, and other inferior officers, ought not onely not to cast the saintes of God in prison (hauing commandement thereunto by the Prince) for feare of loosing their offices: but to withstand euill, to support them, and to deliuer them, to the vttermost of their power. ibid. page 87. 88, 89. 90.

If we see a sheepe in daunger to be deuoured of a wolfe, wee are bounde to deliuer it: euen so to our power wee are bound to put to our hands, to deliuer the children of God, when wee see them pitiouslie in danger, by Gods enemies. ibid. page 90.

It is the office of Councellors, to bridle the affections of Princes and gouernors: Noblemen were first ordained to bridle Princes. Noblemen haue their honour of the people, to reuenge the iniuries of their Kings, and not for their lustie hawking, nimble dicing & carding, singing and dauncing, open bragging & swearing, false flearing and flattering, subtle picking and stealing, cruell polling and pilling, &c. ibid. page 34. page 35. Obedience. page. 107.

The authoritie, which Princes haue, is giuen them from the people: Kings, princes, and gouernours, haue their authoritie of the people: and (vpon occasion) the people may take it away again, Obedience. 25.

ibid.pag.105. *as men may reuoke their proxies and letters of Atturney.*

Goodman, pag. 190. *Subiects do promise obedience, that the Magistrate might help them: which if he doo not, they are discharged of their obedience.*

ibid.pag. 115. 139. *If Magistrates without feare transgresse Gods laws themselues, and command others to doo the like; then haue they lost that honour and obedience, which otherwise their subiectes did owe unto them: and ought no more to be taken for Magistrates, but be examined, accused, condemned, and punished as priuate transgressors.*

Obedience, pag.111. *Iudges ought by the lawe of God, to summon Princes before them, for their crimes: and to proceed against them, as against all other offenders.*

Goodman, 144.145. Obedience, 110. *Euill Princes ought (by the lawe of God) to bee deposed, and inferior magistrates ought chieflie to doo it.* Examples allowed of Kings deposed. *Edward 2. Richard 2. Christierne of Denmarke, &c.*

It is lawfull to kill wicked kings and tyrants: and both by Gods Obedience,99 103. *lawe and mans lawe, Queene Mary ought to haue beene put to* Goodman, pag.99. *death, as being a tyrant, a monster, a cruell beast, &c.* Examples. *The subiects did kill the Queenes highnesse* Athalia: Iehu, *kil-* Obedience, pag.113. *led the Queenes maiestie* Iesabell: Elias, *beeing no magistrate,* ibid.pag. 114. *killed the Queenes maiesties chaplaines,* Baals *priests. These ex-* ibid.pag.115. *amples are left for our instruction. Where this iustice is not executed, the state is most corrupt.*

Goodman, pag.185. *When Magistrates do cease to do their duties,* (in thus deposing or killing of Princes) *the people are as it were without officers: & then God giueth the sword into their hands, & he himself* ibid.pag.180 *is become immediatly their head: for to the multitude a portion of* ibid.pag.184 *the sword of iustice is committed: from the which no person, King* ibid.pag.185 *Queene, or Emperour (being an Idolater) is exempt: he must die the death. The people in the 25. of Numbers, did hang up certain of their heads and captains: which ought to be for euer a perpetuall example of their duetie, in the like defection from God to hang vp such rulers, as shall draw them from him. If neither the infe-*

rior magistrates, nor the greatest part of people will doo their offices: (in punishing, deposing, or killing of Princes) then the minister must excommunicate such a King: any minister may doo it against the greatest Prince. God will send to the rest of the people, (which are willing to doo their duty, but are not able) some Moses *or* Othoniell. *If they know any* Ionathan, *they must goe vnto him to be their Captaine: and he ought not to refuse them. By the worde of God* (in such a defection) *a priuate man (hauing some speciall inward motion) may kill a tyrant: as* Moses *did the Egyptian: as* Phinees *did the lecherous: and* Ahud *did king* Eglon: *or otherwise, a priuate man may doo so, if he be commaunded or permitted by the common-wealth.* Obedience, pag. 115 Obedience, pag. 116. ibid. 18. Goodman, 199. 200. 201. Obedience, pag. 110.

And vnto some obiections that be made to the contrarie, *these answeres are shaped.*

Ob. Be subiect to higher powers: the powers be ordained of God. Goodman, pag, 106.

Ans. *Wicked Kings are not Gods ordinance. Saint* Paule *speaketh of lawfull powers.* Goodman, pag. 111.

Ob. Seruants must be obedient to their Masters, thogh they be froward.

Ans. Paul *speaketh of bondmen, not of subiects obedience.* Obedience, pag 47.

Ob. Peter was commanded to put vp his sword. Goodman, 122.

Ans. *He was a minister, and no magistrate.*

Ob. Christ could haue called for twelue legions of Angels for his defence, if it had beene lawfull to haue vsed force, for the setting vp of the Gospell. Goodman, 119. 120.

Ans. *Christs kingdome was not of this world: he tooke vpon him no temporall sword: but that hindreth not those that haue it.*

Ob. Ieremy was commanded to obey the king of Babel. Goodman, 125. 126.

Ans. *The secret counsell of God was reuealed to him to that effect. It is no generall rule.*

Goodman. 138.139. *Ob. Dauid* said, God forbid that I should touch the anointed of the Lord.

Ans. *It was in his owne priuate cause, and so vnlawfull.*

Goodman. 202,205. *Ob.* Sir *Thomas Wyat* did, as you would haue others to do, &c. but he had no good successe.

Ans. *The goodnesse of his cause is not to be measured by his successe.*

Page 203. *Hee was no traytour, his cause was Gods: and none, but papists and traytours, can iustly accuse him of treason.*

The Councellors and all others, that would be accounted nobles (and tooke not his part) are in very deede traytours to God and Page 206. *his people, and to their countrie.*

Page 207.

The author of the booke of obedience (he should haue sayd of rebellion) endeth his treatise, with significatiō, that Page 137. *the nobilitie of England,* (hee speaketh of them that were in Queen *Maries* daies) *are not to be trusted either by their words, othes, or handwritings, furder then a man doth see, & hear them, & searsely so far.* And *Goodman* likewise, for his conclusion, is most earnest with all english subiectes, that they would put his doctrine in practise, assuring them that in so doing, Pag. 218. if they be cast *in prison with* Ioseph, *to wild beasts with* Dani-

219. ell, *into the sea with* Ionas, *into the dungeon with* Ieremy, *into*

220. *the fiery furnace with* Sidrach, Misach, *&* Abednago, *yet they*

221. *shalbe comforted: whereas if they will not: in seeking to saue their liues, they shall loose them they shall be cast out of the fauor of God, their consciences shall be wounded with hell-like torments, they shall despaire & seeke to hang themselues with* Iudas, *to murther themselues with* Fraunicis Spira; *drowne themselues with Iudge* Hales, *or else fall mad with Iustice* Morgan, *at* Geneua.

This doctrine saith *Whittingham* (afterward vnworthi- In his preface to Goodmans booke. ly *Deane of Durham*) *was approued by the best learned in these parts, meaning* Caluin *and the rest of the* Geneuians. The

English-

Englishmen of name, there at that time, besides *Goodman* and *Whittingham*, were (as I take it) *Anthony Gilby*, *Miles Couerdall*, *Dauid Whitehead*, and sundry others. Who liking the sayde doctrine also exceedingly, were very earnest to haue the *same printed, for the benefite* (as they sayde) *of their brethren in England*. *Whittingham* made a preface to *Goodmans* booke: wherein hee greatly commendeth this doctrine, and writeth thus, in the name (as it seemeth) of all his fellowes there. *We desire that you* (meaning all in *England* and elsewhere, that loue to know the truth and follow it) *should bee perswaded in this trueth*. Againe, *here thou doest heare the* Eternal *speaking by his minister, &c. quickly giue eare and obay, &c.* And again, *If thou wish for Christian liberty, come and see how it may easily be had, &c.* From *Geneua*.

Here it is very material. further to be obserued, that the rest of the learned men, that fled in *Queene Maries* time, as *Iohn Scory*: *William Barlow: Richard Cox*: *Thomas Beacon: Iohn Bale: Iohn Parkhurst*: *Edmond Grindall: Edwine Sandes: Alexander Nowell: Robert Wisdome*: *Iohn Iewell:* & very many more, hauing no great affection to *Geneua*, bestowed themselues in *Germany*, especially at *Zuricke*, *Basill*, and *Franckeford*. These men maintained the reformation of the Church of *England* in *King Edwards* time: they vsed in their holy assemblies, the forme of seruice, and order of ceremonies, which were then established: and they vtterly missliked, & condemned the foresayd propositions, as very seditious & rebellious, according to the iudgement of all the reformed Churches, (for ought I can learne) both in *Germany* and else-where, besides *Geneua* and her offspring.

Besides they of *Franckeford*, (as it appeareth) notwithstanding their griefe, that they were constrained to leaue their country for their conscience: yet in the middest of all their afflictions, they retained such duetifull harts vn-

to

to *Queene Mary*, (imitating therein the Apostles and Disciples of their Maister) as that they coulde not endure to heare her so traduced into all hatred and obloquy, as shee was by the other sort. *Maister Knox*, comming vpon occasion from *Geneua* to *Franckeford*, was by these graue men, accused of *Treason*, (as he himselfe confesseth) for matters that he had published in print, *against their Soueraigne and the Emperor*: and was faine thereupon, for the sauing of his life, to flye thence secretly backe againe to *Geneua*.

Knox hist. pag. 185.

Lastly, by meanes of their disliking of the sayd propositions, and their further course helde in the defence of the foresayde reformation in *England*, against the other mens counterfeit presbyteries: these learned men at *Franckeford*, could haue small reputation with them of *Geneua*. Thus one of that crew then, hath written since of them. *The English Church, which was assembled at Geneua, was seperated from that superstitious and contentious company, that was at Franckford*. And againe, *They were more giuen vnto vnprofitable ceremonies, then to sincere Religion.*

Knox hist. pag 201.

Ibid. pag. 185.

These things I thought meete, for your aduertisement, to set downe, that the propositions precedent might appeare vnto you, not to haue proceeded from any rash or light conceit in our *English* propounders, publishers, and maintainers of them: but that they doo containe their resolute iudgement, agreeable to those points of the *Geneua* resolution, mentioned before out of *Knox* and *Buchanan*.

Whereby it is apparant, that if our sayd *English Geneuians*, had found as redy assistance at that time in *England*, as *Knox* and his complices (about, or soone after the same time) did in *Scotland*, they would not haue fayled, to haue put the sayde positions aswell in practise heere with vs, as some *Scottish* Ministers did in that Country. Which great mischiefe, and disloyall outrage, as the state here, did then

proui-

prouidently suppresse and withstande: So her Excellent Maiesty, hath since preuented, by abolishing of the Romish Religion, and the restoring of the Gospell, which was the quarrell in those dayes pretended. So as our English Reformers, hauing hitherto had no cause for this point to imitate the foresayde proceedinges in *Scotland*, it remayneth, that I shew vnto you, how far (as yet it is disclosed) and how directly they endeuour to follow the said practises of the *Scottish* Ministers, for the erecting vp in *England* of the *Geneua* new Papacie.

CHAP. II.

Our English Disciplinarians, doo imitate the Scottish, in their desire of the Consistoriall gouernement, sauing that they are more bewitched with a kind of dotage after it.

IN *Scotland*, notwithstanding that at the last the Ministers had obtayned, in some sorte, the allowance of the confession of their faith, contayning the summe of that doctrine, which before they had so greatly desired: yet because they wanted the *Geneua* discipline, wherein consisted their very great ioy, together with the hope of their future soueraignety, they were but a little satisfied with all the rest. And euen so, it hath fallen out since in *England*, sauing (for ought I can read) that the sayd *Scottish* ministers were not then come vnto so great a dotage after this Discipline, as there now is growne amongst vs.

About some two or three and forty yeares agone, and after, in the beginning of her Maiesties Raigne, the deuisers themselues of this new platforme, were well content to accept of, and commend such Churches, as had abandoned Popery, though they had withall imbraced ano- Harmonia confess. Cal. Epist. &c.

 ther

ther kinde of Discipline.

Then in disputation against the Papists and Anabaptists, there could bee found in all *Fraunce* and *Geneua*, but two essentiall notes of the Church: vz. *the true preaching of the word, and the right administration of the Sacraments.*

Bertram pa. 15 Mornay p. 37. Caluin instit. lib. 4. Cap. 1. sect. 9. Beza in colloquio Posiaceno. Conuict. de statu Gall. pasto. fol. 122.

Then vpon *Goodmans, Whittinghams*, & *Gilbies* returne, (with the rest of their associates) from *Geneua* into *England:* although it grieued them at the hart, that they might not beare as great a sway here in their seuerall consistories, as *Caluin* did at *Geneua*, and so not onely repined and grudged at her Maiesties reformation of this Church, but laboured (as they might) to sowe abroade in the lande that seede, which hath brought forth a great part of all the disorders, troubles, and disobediences, that since haue ensued. Yet notwithstanding, they meddle not much *in shewe*, (for any thing I can heare of,) with matters of this Discipline, but rather busied themselues, about the apparrell of ministers, ceremonies prescribed, and in picking of quarrels against the common Booke.

This appeareth by their letters, sermons, and by Gilbies most rayling Dialogue betwixt a lame souldier of Barwicke, and an English Captaine.

Confes 5. & 7.

Marry since that, Maister *Beza* deuised a way, howe to bring in the *Geneua* Discipline, to be a third essentiall note of the Church: since, Maister *Cartwright* hath beene at *Geneua*, and vpon his returne did ingage his credit to iustifie that platforme, to be a necessary forme of Gouernement, prescribed by Christ for all times and places: since, Maister *Trauerse* hath also beene there, and did take vpon him in his booke *de Disciplina Ecclesiastica*, to do the like: since, Maister *Cartwright* did likewise (at his second beeing beyonde the seas,) sende vs worde in his second booke, that Master *Beza accounted his sayde third note of the Church*, (*vz. the Geneua* Discipline) *to bee as necessarie a note, as either the word or Sacraments:* and since, Maister *Cartwright* and *Trauers*, with the chiefest of their followers in *England*, haue of

T.C. Second replie pa. 53.

later

later yeares (vpon consideration of the premisses, and further deliberation, in their conferences and meetinges to that purpose) resolued and concluded generally, for the necessity of the same Discipline, which before had beene onely deliuered with vs, as their priuate opinions: Since these times (I say) the friends and fauorers of it, haue from time to time, by certain degrees, so increased in their fond affections towards it; as that now they are in a manner ouercome with the strength and violence of them, and doo bragge in their bookes, that they will not sticke to dye in the cause.

Maister *Cartwright* (as I take it) had an especiall eye to this deuise when he sayth, *that certaine of the things*, which he and his followers do stand vpon, *are such, as if euery haire of their heads, were a seuerall life, they ought to afford them all in defence of them.* Diuers other besides, doo offer *to aduenture their liues for the iustifiyng of it*, as *Vdall* & *Penry*, & nothing will content them without the *Geneua* discipline. For say they, *it is found* [a] *to be the onely bond of peace, the bane of heresie, the punisher of sinne and maintainer of righteousnes.*

Epist. before the demonst.
Epist. before the sup.
a Practise of Prelats D.2.

It is pure, [b] *perfect, and full of all goodnes, for the peace, wealth and honour of Gods people, and is ordained for the ioy and happines of all Nations.*

b Motion. pa. 46.

The want [c] *of the Eldership is the cause of all euill. It is not* [d] *to bee hoped for, that any common-wealth will flourish without it. This Discipline* [e] *is no small part of the Gospell: it is of the substance of it. It is the* [f] *right stuffe & gold for building the Church of God. This would make the* [g] *Church a chast spouse, hauing a wonderfull brightnes as the morning, faire as the Moone, pure as the Sunne, and terrible like an army with banners. Without* [h] *this Discipline, there can be no true Religion. This gouernement* [i] *is the scepter, whereby alone Christ Iesus ruleth among men. The Churches of God in* [k] *Denmarke, Saxony, Tigurin, &c. wanting*

c T. C lib.2. in the Epist.
d T.C.lib. 1. page 3.
e T. C.lib.1. pa.6.and 48.
f Motion 84.
g Ibid. 84.
h Register. p.68.
i Epi before sup. A.2.
k Martin Iunior, Thes, 14.

l T.C.lib.1. pag.3. m T.C.lib. 1.pag.220. n T.C. Table preface to the demonst. o Motion to the Lordes. page 22. p Ibid. pa.49.

this gouernement, are to bee accounted maymed, and vnperfect. The establishing [l] *of the Presbyteries, is the full placing of Christ in his kingdome. They that* [m] *reiect this Discipline, refuse to haue Christ raigne ouer them: and deny* [n] *him in effect, to be their king or their* [o] *Lord. It is the blade* [p] *of a shaken sword, in the hande of the Cherubins, to keepe the way of the tree of life.*

Ridiculous men and bewitched. As though Christs soueraignety, kingdome, and lordship were no where acknowledged, or to be found, but where halfe a dosen artizans, Shoomakers, Tinkers, and Tailors, with their Preacher and Reader, (eight or nine Cherubins forsooth) do rule the whole parish. But I haue noted vnto you, out of these few places, (omitting many other) this their wonderfull dotage, to this end: that it may be considered, whether it be likely, that our *English Consistorians* hauing ouerrunne the *Scottish* ministers, or at the least ouertaken them, in their opinions of the necessity of this Discipline, will be left behind them, in their practises according to the *Geneua* resolution, for the attayning of it, or no.

CHAP. III.

Our pretended English reformers doo imitate or rather exceede the Scottish Ministers in rebelling and rayling against all that doo encounter them.

WHen in *Scotland* they first had in minde to reforme religion, and after to erect their Discipline, (according to the *Geneua* resolution) they spent their wittes and all their deuises, by railing and slandering, to bring the *Bishoppes* and the rest of the Clergy, with the whole course of their gouernements into detestation and hatred with the people. *They write their*

owne

owne pleasures of them, and to them: and that in the name of the people. They stirred the Nobility *by their writings against them: they had their supplications to their Parliaments: and to the Queene Regent; they had their appellations from their Bishops, their exhortations to the Nobility, to the Estates and comminalty*, and many such practises they had to that purpose, yea, after their *Bishops* and *Clergy* had receiued the Gospell.

Knox hist. pag 234. ibid. pag. 213, 214, 216. ibid. pag. 256. ibid. pag. 304.

But in this course, our reformers in *England*, haue not onely imitated them, but (as ready Schollers, and apt for such mischiefe) haue very farre exceeded both them, and as I thinke) all others, that hitherto haue dealt that way. They haue renued ouer againe, & applied to our Church gouernours, two or three of the most bitter Treatises, that euer were made against the *Popes, Cardinals, Popish Bishops*, Monkes and Friers, &c. in *King Henry* the eight his dayes. They haue foure or fiue very diuellish and infamous *Dialogues*: likewise their *complaints* and *petitions* to her Maiesty and Parliament, in the name of the *comminalty*, their *appellation*, their *exhortation*, and diuers other most lewd & scurrilous Epistles and Letters.

Sathan prince of hell, to the *Pope*, Cardinals, Bishopes, &c. *Practise of Prelates*. 1. Gilbies. 2. *I.B.* 3. Vdals. 4. That which came from Throgmor.

When they are called before any Magistrate, and dealt withall for their factious proceedings, they vsually afterward doo take vpon them to write and publish, vnder the name of a conference, what wordes and arguments haue passed: which they perfourme with all reproch, disdaine, vntruth, and vanity: and so do pester the Realme and their fauourers closets, with infinite such shamelesse and slaunderous discourses, as is most intollerable.

They haue had fiue or sixe *supplications* to seuerall *Parliaments*, penned altogether according to *Knox* his stile and violent spirit, in many places word for word: besides *Martin*, and his two sonnes, their holy imitations of *Beza* his Passauantius, (that all things might proceede *Geneua* like) in

Martins Epi. His Epitome. Hay any wor. Martin Iuni. *Martin* Senior Martin *Prote.*

in their sixe bookes of *Consistorian* grauity. And now, vpon better care taken by her Maiesty, that no such libels should be hereafter printed in *England*, (at the least without some daunger to the parties, if it may bee knowne) they haue founde such fauour, as to procure their chiefe instrument and old seruant *Waldgraue*, to be the King of *Scots* Printer, from whence their wants in that behalfe shall be fully supplyed.

Refor. no enemie.

For hauing obtained that place, (as hee pretendeth in Print) they haue published by hundreths, certaine spitefull and malicious bookes against her Maiesties most honorable priuy Councell. Also their *humble motion* to their LL[s]. with three or foure other very slanderous Treatises. And now it seemeth, for feare that any of all their sayd Libels & rayling Pamphlets, (that haue bin written in her highnesse time) should perish, (being many of them but triobolar chartals:) they haue taken vpon them to make a *Register*: and to Print them altogether in *Scotland*, in two or three volumes: as it appeareth by a part of the sayde *Register*, all ready come from thence, and finished: which containeth in it three or foure and forty of the sayd Libels.

In all which courses taken, more then heathnish, this is their drift and especiall end, that hauing by their forged lies, their poysoned tongues, and their hypocriticall outcries, procured a generall mislike of her *Maiesties* reformation, the present gouernment of the *Church*, the chiefest defender thereof, the Lords that fauour it, the *Archbishops* and *Bishops* that haue authoritie in it, & the rest of the Clergy that doe submit themselues vnto it: they might come at the last to attaine their purpose, and by fishing in our troubled waters, (according to the *Geneua* resolution) set vp and establish their glorious scepter and kingdome.

Out of these bookes, because some might otherwise

charge

charge the premises herein with slander of the godly brethren, I haue thought it very conuenient to lay downe before you, particularly, some most lewd and wicked speeches, in maner and order, as in tenne of the next Chapters following, is specified.

Chap. IIII.

The speaches of the said pretended reformers, concerning England: the state, the present reformation, and gouernment of the Church.

Ngland [a] *with an impudent forehead, hath sayd: I will not come neare the holy one. And as for the building of his house, I will not so much as lift vp a finger towardes that worke, nay I will continue the desolations thereof.* [b] *England hateth them to this day, that faithfullie doe their office. Of* [c] *all the nations that haue renounced that whore of* Rome, *there is none in the world so farre out of square, as England, in retaining the Popish Hierarchy.*

a Penries Epistle before the humble motion.

b Gilby, p.77

c Epistle before the demonst. B.3.

We in [d] *England are so farre off, from hauing a Church rightly reformed, that as yet we are scarse come to the outward face of the same. We* [e] *are neuer the better for her Maiesties reformation, seeing the walles of* Syon *lie euen with the ground* (that is, seeing their discipline, is not established.)

d 1. Adm.p.4

e Supplica. to the Parliament, pag.67

Your [f] *reformation* (as it standeth) *will be little better, then that of the Samaritanes, who feared* Iehouah: *but worshipped their owne Gods. Men* [g] *belike doe thinke no more to be required at their handes, then the rasing of Babell: the diuell as yet contenting himselfe with Bethel. Your* [h] *gouernment is that, which giueth leaue to a man to be anie thing, sauing a sound Christian.* Omnia cum liceant, non licet esse bonum.

f Supplica.62

g Supplica.68

h Preface to the demonst. A.4.

We

i 1.Adm.pa.2. k Epist. before the supplica. l 1. Adm.p.25 m Gilbyes dial.151. n 1 Adm.p.33. o Suppl. to the Parlia, 56. p Hay any.pa, 5,6,8,12. q Martins Epistle.33. r Hay any, pa. 13.

We [i] lacke a right gouernement of the Church. In [k] stead of the ordinance of God in the gouernment of his Church, the marchandize of shamelesse Babylon is maintayned. The [l] gouernment now vsed by Archbishops, Bishops, &c. is both Antichristian and diuelish. Rome is [m] come home to our gates. Antichrist [n] raigneth amongst vs. The [o] established gouernement of the Church, is trayterous against the maiestie of Iesus Christ: it confirmeth the Popes supremacie, it is accursed. It is [p] an vnlawfull, a false, a bastardly gouernement. In the state of the Church there is nothing [q] but sores and blisters, yea the griefe is euen deadly at the heart: They [r] must needes be not onely traytors to God and his word, but also enemies vnto her Maiestie, and the land, that defend the established gouernement of the Church to be lawfull.

Chap. V.

Some of their vndutifull and consistorian speeches concerning her Maiesty, &c.

a Martins Epistle 10,53. b Hay any, page 5. c Ibid pag. 13 15,23. d Register, pa. 48. e Gilbyes preface to his dialogue of the souldier of Barwicke.

T*He [a] Bishoppes haue long deceaued,* and *seduced her Maiestie and her people. Doo [b] you thinke our Church gouernement to bee good and lawfull, because her Maiesty and the state, who maintaine the reformed religion, alloweth the same? why? the Lord doth not allow it.* In effect: *that [c] her Maiesty and state, (in maintaining the established gouernement, and reiecting theirs) doo mayme and deforme the body of Christ, and so doo bid God to battell against them. Ministers [d] ought not to obey the Prince, when he prescribeth ceremonies, and a fashion of apparell. By [e] the same authority, that the Queene commandeth the apparell, now appointed to the Ministers, she may commaund any piece of Popery, so she name it pollicie.* Achaz, *of pollicie, brought such an altar into Ierusalem, as he did see at Damascus, where he had ouercome the Idolaters and their Idols. But cursed*

was

was his policie, and so are all they that retaine any thing of their old Idolatrie, (he addeth for example, *the candlestickes vpon the Queenes altar, kneeling at the communion, &c.*)[f] *Of necessitie, all Christian magistrates are bound to receiue this gouernement by Pastors, Doctors, Elders and Deacons, and to abolish all other Church gouernement.* [g] *Either her Maiestie knoweth not what they desire, being abused by the Bishops; or else shee is negligent of her dutie, and vnthankefull to God.*

f Martin Iunior. Thes.22

g Motion out of Scotland to the Lords. pag.41.

Her [h] Maiestie, is cunninglie resembled, to *Ieroboam, Ahab, Iehoram, Ahaz, Gedeon, Nadab, Saule, Iehu, Asa, and Iehosaphat* in those points, whereby they offended God, and she is threatned by their examples, in that hauing begon so well, she doth not proceede to set vp Christes gouernment throughly.

h Gilbie,66. 68 142. Motion.p.31. 32.33.

A question being asked (as the register reporteth) by the Bishop of London, Anno. 1567. vz. *haue we not a godly Prince? speake: is shee euill?* There are three answers made, by three seuerall men. The first: *what a question is that? the fruites do shew.* The second: *No. But the seruants of God are persecuted vnder her.* The thirde: *Why: this question the Prophet answereth in the Psalmes: how can they haue vnderstanding that worke iniquitie, spoiling my people, and that extoll vanitie?* To this obiection: that *it is*[k] *Dotanisme to challenge such authoritie ouer Princes,* (meaning the authority which the Eldership challengeth) answere is made: vz *It is flatterie to suffer Princes to do what they list.*

i Regist.p 33.

Wil. Why. Tho. Rowlãd Ro. Hawkins

k Demonst. of Discipline. pag 75.

To this[l] position: *That princes should bee excepted from Ecclesiasticall Discipline, and namely from excommunication,* they answere thus. *That excommunication should not be exercised against Princes, I vtterlie mislike:* To affirme that, *It is but a meere mockerie of the Lord, and to offer himselfe* (meaning the now *L. Archbishop of Canterbury*) *as a bawd to al maner of sinnes in Princes.* To *insinuate, that others being subiect*

l T. C. 2 part of his 2 replie pag. 65.

ibid.pag.92.

to this correction, onelie Princes should be exempted, (I feare,) commeth from a worse cause, then from simple error.

Chap. VI.

Some of their rayling speaches against the high court of Parliament; and all others generally that do maintaine the present gouernment of the Church of England.

For not admitting the platforme set downe in the first admonition, &c. Anno. 14. of her Maiestie: and suffering the parties, that offered, it to be punished: Thus they write. *The* [m] *state sheweth it selfe not vpright, alledge the Parliament what it will: al honest men shall finde lacke of equitie; all good consciences shall condemne that Court. It shalbe easier for* Sodom *and* Gomorrha, *in the day of iudgement, then for such a Court. There is no other thing to be looked for, then some speedie vengeance to light vpon the whole land, prouide aswell as the politicke Machiauels of England thinke they can though God do his worst.*

m 2. Admonition pag, 3

Likewise of the Parliament, the 29. of her Maiestie (for their tollerating the Bishops, &c. in stead of their newe gouernment) it is said. That they shalbe in danger *of* [n] *the terrible masse of Gods wrath, both in this life and in the life to come:* and that if they did not then abrogate (the gouernment by Bishops,) *well* [o] *they might hope for the fauor and intertainement of* Moses *(that is the curse of the law,) but the fauour and louing countenance of Iesus Christ, they should not see nor euer enioy.*

n Supl. pa. 18,

o Sup pa, 25

Againe of the same Parliament, it is likewise affirmed: that (if the reformation desired, were not graunted,) *they*

should

should betray God, betray the truth, and betray the whole kingdome. They [q] *should declare themselues to be an assembly, wherein the Lordes cause could not be heard; an assembly, wherein the felicity of miserable men could not be respected; an assembly, that wittingly called for the iudgements of God vpon the whole land; an assembly, wherein trueth, religion, and pietie could beare no sway: There* [r] *shalbe not be a man of their seede that shall prosper be a Parliament-man, or beare rule in England any more.*

q ibid, pag, 7

r Ibid, pag, 43

Furthermore, a prophesie is passed (but from that spirit, I trust that tooke vpon him to be, *spiritus mendax in ore prophetarum*) that if they preuailed not in the said Parliament according to their supplication: *then* [s] *the Nauie of the Spaniards should come againe, and fight against this land, and waste it with fire and sworde: that God shal send a terror into the harts of our valiantest and stoutest men: that one enemie shall chase a thousand of vs: & that although we had smit the whole hoast, so as there remayned none but wounded men amongst them, yet shal euerie man rise vp in his tent, and ouerrunne this land.*

1 Of the kings. 22.

s Sup, pag, 75 76.

Lastly, this they write generally, of al that do withstād their desires: *Those* [t] *kingdomes and states who defend anie Church gouernement, saue this of Pastors, Doctors, Elders, and Deacons, are in danger of vtter destruction. None* [u] *euer defended this Hierarchy of Bishops to be lawfull, but Papistes, and such as were infected with Popish errors. No* [x] *man can open his mouth* (against Presbiteries) *but with a shamelesse face, and seared conscience. The* [y] *enemies hereof after the manner of the wicked, mentioned in* Iob, *do say vnto the almighty, depart from vs. because we desire not the knowledge of thy waies: yea and in their practise they say, who is the almighty, that we should serue him?*

t Martin iunior: Thes. 28

u ibid, Th. 46

x Motion out of Scotland, pag, 20

y Epistle to the suppl, A, 3

This [a] *shalbe the portion, of as many, as (to the end) oppose themselues against the cause of reformation now laboured for: the heauen shall declare his wickednesse, and the earth shall rise*

a Epist, to the Sup. A 4,

 vp

vp against him: the encrease of his house shall goe away: it shall flow away in the day of his wrath: his eyes shal see his destruction, and he shall drinke of the wrath of the Almighty. Th y [b]are no better to bee thought of, then enemies to the Gospell of Christ, to her Maiestie, and people: that seeke to keepe Christes holy Discipline from amongst vs. This [c]is that cause, against which neuer man yet striued and prospered. All the Newgates and Oldgates, yea and all the Tiburns in England, are too little for such rash, and presumptuous heades, that will not giue God leaue to rule: but will take the scepter out of his handes. I do [e] feare that many of the forwardest ennemies of reformation, are not the backwardest frendes, that the king of Spain hath in England at this day.

b Register out of Scotland. pa.71.
c. Epi before the supl.
d Exhort to the BB.B, I,
e Penry in his Epi. from Scotl. before reformat. no ennemie

CHAP. VII.

Some of their Disciplinarian speeches concerning the Lordes of her Maiesties most honorable priuie Councell.

OVr [f] Councell may truelie be saide, to delight in the iniury & violent oppression of Gods saincts & Ministers: therefore the Lord wil surely visite our Councel, with an heauie plague.

Our Councel [g] cannot possibly deale truely in matters of iustice, betweene man and man; insomuch as they bend all their forces, to bereaue Iesus Christ of his gouernment. The which vngodly and wicked course as they haue held on, euer since the beginning of her Maiesties raigne: so at this day they haue taken great boldnesse, and growne more rebellious, against the Lord and his cause, then euer they were. In so much as their honors, in token of thankefulnesse to him that exalted them: dare now charge the cause of reformation, to be an ennemie vnto our state and such as fauor the same, to be vnquiet and factious men, disturbers

f Epist. from Scotl. before reformat. no ennemie. A.3.
g Ibid. A 3. & 4

disturbers of the common peace and quietnes, and sowers of sedition among the subiects.

They do [h] *notablie detect their impiety against God, and their enmitie to the kingdome of his Sonne Christ: they offer iniury to her Maiestie. If her Maiesty giue eare to such Councellors, shee may haue cause one day to lament. Assuredly, those that are our ennemies for the profession of the truth,* (meaning the pretended Discipline(*cannot bee her Maiesties sure frendes, whatsoeuer they pretend.* h Ibid,A,4

Sathan [i] *worketh the defacing of the way of truth: & supporteth his owne kingdome, by instruments of no meane countenance.* i,Ibid,A,4

Be they noble or [k] *vnnoble, Councellors or inferior men: I am so farre from fearing their power, that the more I see them rage, the greater strength I haue, to stand to the truth, which they raue against.* k, Ibid,B,1

I do warne [l] *and admonish those Councellors, with whome and against whome especially, I deale in this Treatise, to repent them of their great insolencie, whereby they haue beene puffed vp with Senacharib, to magnifie and oppose themselues; against the cause and people of the Lord of Hosts: as against the Religion and people, of some of the Gods of the earth. Otherwise they are to feare least the Lord, hauing raised vp many of them, out of mean places into the throne of iustice, meaneth to shew his power and great name, by making them examples of his fearefull wrath; as he did Pharaoh, who wrought his owne ouerthrow.* l. Ibid, B 1.

m, Ibid, B, 1

If men will wonder, that [m] *we being so contemptible in the sight of the world, dare yet be so bold, as to controll great states and mightie men; and to chalenge them of iniustice, against the Sonne of God and his members; who will not sticke to brag with Pilate, that they haue power to crucifie Christ, & to absolue him; they are to vnderstand, that wee know of no power, but from aboue: and therefore of no power, that is able to beare out iniustice and wrong. The hils of the Robbers wee grant to bee high, and vnassayleable in the sight of an eye of flesh: but we haue learned of the holy man, to account the habitation of the wicked to be accursed, euen when hee seemeth to be best rooted: for we know that the steppes of his strength, shall bee restrayned, and that his Counsaile shall cast him downe.*

Chap. VIII.

Some of their rayling speeches against the Magistracy in England, the Iudges, Lawyers, and lawes both ciuill and ecclesiasticall.

n Epist. from Scotl. before reformat. no ennemie. A, 3.

THen [n] Magistracy and ministery haue walked hand in hand, in the contempt of true Religion: and vnto both, the worde of the Lorde is made a reproch.

o Ibid. A. 3.

Amongst [o] those who deale in the cause of iustice, there are found wicked persons: euen wicked lawyers and iudges, (who seeme to know of no other God, but their owne gaine, (that lay waite for the blood of Gods saints, as hee that setteth snares; and marke whether they can heare of any, that go further in the cause of God, then the corruption of our state doth permit. And if they finde any such, they know how to wrest against them, a clause of some statute, contrary not onely to the meaning thereof, but euen contrary vnto all iustice and equity, yea common reason it selfe, and the verie groundes of all good lawes and statutes. So that it is now growen, and hath bene of a long time, a common practise of these Godlesse men, to make of the statutes, ordained for the maintenance of Religion and common quietnesse, a pit, wherein to catch the peaceable of the land.

p ibid. A. 3

The common [p] inditements of the Lords true and faithfull Ministers, for matters of trifles, as the omission of the surplisse, churching of women, crosse in Baptisme, &c. doth manifestly witnesse the iniquitie of these Atheists.

The

The [q] lawes, that maintaine the Archbishops and Bishops are no more to bee accounted of, then the lawes maintaining the Stewes. q Maitin Iunior. Thes. 34:

The [r] humaine lawes, that maintaine them, are wicked and vngodly. r ibid. Thes. 38.

The lawes [s] are made their common sanctuarie, to defend all our wickednesse. s Fenner against Bridges, p, 5.

Impiety is [t] suffered to beare sway against the maiestie of God: and that by law and authority. t Sup. pa. 59

Such lawes [u] are retayned in force, as iustle and ouerthrow the royall prerogatiue of the sonne of God. v Sup, pa, 24,

As [x] great indignity is offered vnto Iesus Christ, in committing his Church vnto the gouernement of the common law, as can be, by meane hyrelings vnto a king: in committing his beloued spouse vnto the direction of the mistresse of the Stewes, and enforcing her to liue after the lawes of a brothel-house. x Epistle before the demonst. B. 4

Chap. IX.

Some of their consistoriall sayings, as touching our Religion, Communion booke, Sacraments and Ceremonies.

E [a] striue for true religion. As [b] our lackes are, there can be no right religion. [c] Many religions are mixed together, of Christ and Antichrist, of God and the deuill. [d] Christes Religion is fondly patched with the Popes; ioyning fire and water, heauen and hel together. The [e] truth (in a manner) doth but peepe out from behinde the screene.

a 1 Adm. 32,
b ibid, pag, 2.
c Gilby, p. 29.
d. ibid. pag. 90
e, 2, Adm, p 6

Their [f] prescript forme of seruice, is full of corruption. In [g] all the order of their seruice, there is no edification, but confusion. The [h] Communion booke is an vnperfect booke, culled and picked out of that popish dunghill, the portuise and masse-booke: and

f 1. Adm, p, 17
g ibid, pag. 24
h ibid, pag, 16

and many of the contents therein be such, as are against the word of God. And [i] *Martin senior* calleth *it our sterue-vs Booke.*

i Martin senior. C. 2.

The [k] *Sacraments are wickedlie mangled and prophaned. They* [l] *eate not the Lords supper but play a pageant of their own, to blinde the people: and keepe them still in superstition: to make the seely soules beleeue that they haue an English masse: and so put no difference betwixt trueth and falsehoode, betwixt Christ and Antichrist, betwixt God and the deuill.* [m] *The publike baptisme is full of childish and superstitious toyes.*

k 2 Admon. pag. 42.
l Gilby, pag. 2

m 1 Admon pag. 21.

And of our orders, garments, and ceremonies. They are [n] *carnall, beggerly: Antichristian pompes, rites, lawes, and traditions: popish fooleries, Romish reliques, & rags of Antichrist dregs and remnants of transformed Poperie: Pharisaicall outward faces and vizardes: remnants of Romish Antichrist: of superstition, and Idolatrie: Knowne liueries of Antichrist: accursed leauen of the blasphemous Popish Priesthoode: cursed patches of Poperie and Idolatrie, they are worse then Lowsie: for they are sib be to the sarke of* Hercules, *that made him teare his owne bowels asunder.*

n Gilby. p. 40. pag. 41. Pag. 1 pag. 5. pag. 12. pag. 14. pag. 91. pag. 96. pag 95 pag. 150

Chap. X.

How they charge the present gouernment with persecution.

o 2. Admon pag. 59

p, ibid.

Here [o] *is a persecution of poore Christians, & the professors of the Gospell suffred, not far vnlike to the six articles. Gods* [p] *cause is troden vnder foote, and the benefite of his Church is little regarded.*

q 1 Adm. p. 2

r Practise of Prelates. D, 8

[q] *Poore men haue been miserably handled, with reuilings, depriuations, imprisonments, bannishments, and such like extremities. Godly* [r] Ministers *haue beene brought before the barres of iustice: they haue beene arraigned amongst fellons and theeues: they haue been imprisoned to the vttermost and defaced: they are reproched*

reproched, shaken up, threatened; many are depriued : they are examined by an inquisition, much like that of Spaine. O lamentable case, O heynous impietie.

[s] shal they be thus marked with the blacke cole of reproach & villanie? O inhumaine and more then barbarous impietie. s ibid B.2

Besides [t] whorish impudencie, halter, axe, bandes, scourging, and racking, our Bishops haue nothing to defend themselues withall. t Mart protest. 13.

The [u] Clinke, Gatehouse, White-Lion, and the Fleete, are their onelie arguments. u Vdal.dialogue. F,1

If [a] Isay, Ieremie, Ezechiel, Osee, Micheas, and Zacharie, were aliue: they would be carried to the Marshall-sea, the White-lyon, the Kings-bench, the Gate-house, and other Prisons, yea to Newgate. a Exhorta, to BB. A.1

In [b] effect, as Caine persecuted Abell: Esau, Iacob: the Patriarches, their brother Ioseph, the Iewes, Moses: the Priests Ieremie, Osea, Amazia and Christ: euen so in these dayes, the Preachers are slandred and persecuted by such, as would seeme pillars of true religion. If this persecution[c] be not prouided for, it is the case of many a thousand in England, greate trobles will come of it. b 2, Admon. pag. 1. & 2. c pag. 59.

The [d] land is sore troubled: there is no place nor being, for a faithfull Minister of the word. Our bloud crieth for vengeance against the Bishops. d Dialog that came from Throg, D.2

I [f] am made like to our Sauiour Christ who hath troden this path, in that (as he sayth) hee is troubled not for euiil, but for good, It fares [g] with vs as with [prisoners in Poperie: God sende vs their comfort, Ministers [h] are in worse sort suppressed now, then they were by the Papists in Queene Maries time. This crosse [i] is common, not onelie with him, but with all that will liue godly in Christ. The cause is holy: and his sufferinges acceptable. I [k] perceiue the Lyon roareth, but cannot bite, further then the Lord shall permit. e Martin. protest. pag, 9 f Snape to his father, 1590. g Wight before he was imprisoned to a frend. h Lord in his papers. i Fen of Lords imprisonmēt.

CHAP. XI.

Some of their Consistorian speeches of the Clergie of England, assembled, as occasion hath required, in the Conuocation house.

Sup. pa. 47.

Hey[1] are wolues. It is a Synagogue. Their onely endeuour is, how to preuent Christ, from bearing rule in the Church, by his own lawes. They are knowne to bee ennemies vnto all sinceritie. The whole conuocation house, are (in iudgement) contrarie to our Sauiour Christ, they are intollerable oppugners of Gods glory: and vtter ennemies vnto the liberties of his Church. As long as that house standeth, (as at this day it doth) there can be no hope at al, that either Gods heauenlie trueth, should haue free passage, or the Church her libertie, in this kingdom. They haue seduced and deceiued the ciuil state, & people, in bearing them in hand, that al is wel in the Church.

Pag. 48. pag 49. pag. 53 pag. 55.

They are termed, (by one of the [m] Captaines of this crue) *right puissant, poisoned, persecuting, and terrible Priests: Clergie maisters of the confocation house: the holie league of subscription: the crue of monstrous and vngodlie wretches: that mingle heauen and earth together: horned maisters of the conspiration house: an Antichristian swinish rabble: ennemies of the Gospell: most couetous, wretched and Popish Priests, the Conuocation house of Diuels Belzabub[n] of Canterbury, the chiefe of the Diuels.*

m, Mart, Epist

n Dialogue that came from Throgmort. D.4

CHAP. XII.

Some of their presbiterial speeches of the Bishops of England professing the Gospell.

o Hay any. p. 15.14, &c.

He [o] Bishops are the greatest and most pestilent ennemies that now our state hath, & are like to be the ruine of her Maiestie

Maiestie, and the whole state: Archbishops and Bishops are vnlawfull, vnnaturall, false, and bastardlie gouernours of the Church, and the ordinances of the Diuel: pettie Popes: pettie Antichristes: like incarnat Diuels: they are Bishops of the Diuell: Bishops[p] are cogging and coosening knaues. They will lie like dogs. Our [q] Bishops are proud, popish, presumptuous, prophane, paltrie, pestilent, pernicious prelates, & vsurpers: Impudent, shamelesse, and waynescot faced Bishops, like beastes. They are in a premunire. They ought not to bee maintayned, by the authority of the ciuill Magistrate, in any common wealth. They[r] are, in respect of their places, ennemies of God. The [s] worst Puritane is an honester man, then the best Lord Bishop in Christendome.

pag. 20. pag. 21 Idid, 28. p Martins Epist. 37. q Epist, pag. 6 pag. 33. pag. 21 pag. 4 r Vdals dialogue. c. 1 s Martins protest. 27.

Their[t] crueltie is without measure. They are butchers and horseleeches: it is the portion of their inheritance. Their bloudthirstie attempts. These dragons. Their tirannie and bloudthirstie proceedings are inexcusable. In effect, that they conspire to pull the Crowne from her Maiesties head.

t Martins, protest, pag. 4. pag. 8. pag. 12 pag, 21 pag, 21

Bishops[u] callings are meere Antichristian. The[x] Bishops are robbers, Wolues, simoniacks, persecutors, sowers of sedition and discontentednes betweene her Maiesties subiectes. They haue incurred the statute of premunire: they are (ipso facto) depriuable. Though they bee in the Church, yet are they none of the Church. The true Church of God ought to haue no more to doe with them, and the Synagogue, (namely their Antichristian Courts) them with the Synagogue of Sathan. Be[a] packing Bishops: you striue in vaine, you are laid open already. Friers and Monkes were not so bad.

u Vdals dialogue. D, 2 x Martin sen. B. 4. c. 1 a Epist to the epitom.

Of[b] all the Bishops that euer were in the See of the Archbishop of Canterburie, there was neuer any did so much hurt to the Church of God as hee hath done. No Bishop that euer had such an aspiring and ambitious minde as hee, no not Cardinall Wolsey. None so proud as he: No not Stephen Gardiner of Winchester

b The Dialog that came from Throgmort, D. 3

c Ibid, C.4.

ster. None so tirannicall as he: no not Bonner. He sits[c] vpon his cogging stoole, which may truelie be called, the chaire of pestilence. His mouth is full of cursing against God and his Saintes. His feete are swift to shed bloud: there is none of Gods children, but had as leeue see a Serpent, as meete him. It grieueth them to see so wicked an ennemie of God and his Church. Belsebub[d] of Canterbury. The Canterburie Caiphas: Esau: a monstrous Antichristian Pope: a most bloudie oppressor of Gods Saintes: a very Antichristian beast: a most vile and cursed tyrant. In[e] respect of his Antichristian prelacie ouer Gods Church, and for the notable hatred, which he hath euer bewrayed towardes the Lord and his truth, I thinke him one of the dishonorablest creatures vnder heauen.

Mart, sen. C. 1

d Mart sen.

e Epistle out of Scotl. before reforma. no ennemie.

And againe of the Bishops, but especially of the Lord Archbishop. *In[f] his behauiour, wrath, anger, reproch, and disdaine (as in a wood, so manie Lions, Beares, Tigers, and cruell beastes) were seene to range, and in this more sauage, that whereas they by time and vsage may be tamed and appeased, this man neuer. It[g] would be knowen, whether they haue some secret meaning, if oportunitie would serue to aspire vnto the Crowne.*

f Practise of Prelates. C. 6.

g Supp. 37.

Chap. XIII.

Some of their vncharitable wordes against all the Clergie in England, generally that mislike their designements.

WE[h] lacke in England a right ministery of God. The[i] Ministers are neither prooued, elected, called, nor ordeyned according to Gods word. I. B. is to be[k] inuested into the place of a naturall foole, after a solemne manner, according to the booke of ordayning Bishops and Priests.

h 1, Adm. p. 2

i Ibid, pag. 4.

k Mar Iu, C, 2

The

The [l] Clergie is indicted, as the followers of Antichrist, and that their Ministerie is from the Pope. Little [m] or nothing is required of our English Priests; but to say the Catechisme, and to weare a cap, coap, and tippet: Antichrists rags shall make him a Priest, be he neuer such a dolt or a villaine. l Exhort. to BBs, B. 2. m Gilby. p 50 Ibid. pag, 3.

The [n] most part of our Ministers, are either Popish Priestes, or Monkes, or Fryers, or ale-house haunters, or boyes and lads, dronkardes and dolts: that wil weare a fooles hood, for liuing sake: They are Hogges, Dogges, Wolues, Foxes, Simoniakes, Vsurers: procters of Antichrists inuentions: Popish chapmen, halting Newtrals. They seeke nothing, but like greedy dogges, how to fill their paunches. n, Gil, p. 111. pag. 53. pag. 32, pag. 89, pag. 112,

Our supposed Ministers are a multitude of desperate and forelorne Atheists, a cursed, vncircumcised, and murthering generation, you shall finde amongst this crue nothing else, but a troope of bloudy soule-murtherers, and sacreligious Churchrobbers. Bene quod malitia non habet tantas vires, quantos conatus. Epist. from Scotl. before reformat. no ennemie. A. 3. Hier. lib. 2. con Rufin.

Chap. XIIII.

Their especiall drift in their saide railing speeches, as outragiously published, as if they were meere Iesuites, and peraduenture to as dangerous a purpose.

BY the former so wicked and slaunderous speeches, contayned in the tẽ last Chapters, you see how the brotherhood endeuoreth with the multitude, (as I saide) not onely the disgrace of our Church and Clergie men, but likewise how bold they are with her most excellent Maiesty: the high Court of Parliament, the Lords of her priuy Councel: the Iudges lawyers, lawes, and all thinges besides, that do giue any im-

impediment vnto their deuises and complots.

Harding, Dorman, Stapleton, Sanders, Allen, Gregorie Martin, and diuers other fugitiues and Traytors, to make a more easie way, for the bringing in againe of popery: haue taken the like course in her Highnesse time: meaning principally, by such vile slaunders, to withdraw her Highnesse subiects, from their dutifull approbation of the present estate and reformation of Religion.

Goodman, Wittingham, Gilby, the author of the booke of obedience, with the rest of the *Geneua* complices in Queene *Maries* dayes, practised the very same pollicie: when (as you haue heard) according to the *Allobrogicall* resolution, they vrged all states, by degrees, rather to take armes, and to reforme Religion themselues by force, then to suffer such Idolatrie and superstition to remaine in the land.

But in these more political then Christian practises; as I said, that our English *Disciplinarians* of these dayes, haue farre exceeded the *Scottish* Ministers: so may it bee truely affirmed of them, that al the popish Traitors, that hitherto haue written, and all the said *Geneuians* that then liued, for malitious and spitefull tauntes, for rayling and bitter tearmes, for disdaineful and contemptuous speeches, did not come neere them.

Besides, it is especially to be obserued, that in their own opinions, they haue by these vngodly meanes so preuayled with the multitude, as that now they begin to vaunt and bragge of their good successe, already therein attayned. One of them sendeth vs word from *Scotland*, that such as haue withstood their pretended Church gouernment, *are made already in England to bee despised and vile before all the people: that a poore simple Minister of theirs &c. is hearde with more reuerence, and resorted vnto with more diligence*

The Motion. pag. 40. 42.

gence, then one of ours; though he haue the great bell rong, and men to helpe him vp into the pulpit: that this was wrought by a contemptible, and very base and straunge meanes, (meaning Martin and his sonnes libels, &c.) *not once dreamed off by a thousand of Gods saintes: and that when their creastes,* (meaning the Bishops) *were set vp, and they began to say all is ours; then their presumption was dashed, daunted, and taken downe.*

They might as well haue signified vnto vs, in what tearmes and reputation, her Maiestie, her Parliaments, her Lords, her Iudges, and her lawes, do stand and hold with the people. In dealing as they haue done, by their particular supplications and motions vnto her Highnes, and vnto their LL[s]. their intents to that purpose, when the time shall serue (if in the meane while they be not preuented) are notablie disclosed. For otherwise, it might haue sufficed them, to haue deliuered their discontentments, in priuate manner, by writing, both to her Maiestie, their LL[s]. and other in authority: thereby to haue discharged their consciences without their publishing of them in Printe to the world, except their purpose had likewise beene, by that lewd meanes, to haue brought them all into contẽpt, as well as the Bishops. What priuate man, if his friend should write a letter vnto him, and lay open in the same, (eyther truely or falsely) many great crimes to his charge: & afterward should by Printing or any other waies publish it: could otherwise account of his dealing therein, but that he meant to make him thereby odious to the world, or at the least to be of no great account, or estimation.

Queene *Marie* was of nature & disposition, very mild and pitifull; and yet, because shee suffered such crueltie & superstition to be practised & maintained in her days, you haue

haue heard by the consistorian propositions (before mentioned) what was resolued by *Goodman, Whittingham, Gilby*, & the rest of the *Geneuians* against her, concerning her deposition, &c. Which is a matter that would be wel considered-of, and in time prouided-for accordingly: conside-ring that these our home-bred Sicophantes, men of the *Geneua* mould, as proud and presumptuous as any that euer liued, do charge the present state, vnder her Maiestie, (as before it is noted) with such great impietie, corruption, idolatrie, superstition, and barbarous persecution: Which may touch her highnesse, as neerely (by their doctrine) for maintayning the present state, as Queene *Marie* was, for defending of Poperie.

Well the conclusion of this Booke is this, vz: that seeing our *English consistorians* do labour more vehemently, or at the least as egerly, *per fas & nefas*, by slaunder, reproch, and malitious practises, to discredit all those, that withstand them, in their desires, for the *Geneua*-like discipline: as any other *Scottish* Ministers, Papistes, or old *Geneuians*, haue laboured to discredit those, that maintayned al kind of Popery, Idolatry, and superstition; it is to be feared, least they proceede in the *Geneua* Resolution, as their fellowes (whō they do imitate in Scotland, or rather whom they do excell) haue done before them.

The end of the second Booke.

THE

THE THIRD BOOKE OF DISCIPLINARY GROVNDES and Practises.

CHAP. I.

The practises of certaine English Reformers for Discipline, from the yeare, 1560. vntill the yeare, 1572.

AS in *Scotland*, when they could not obtaine their desires, for the full establishing of their booke of Discipline, by lawfull authority; they procured such priuate subscription therunto, as they were able, and so fell themselues to the practise of it (as it hath beene said in the sixt chapter of the first Booke: euen so haue our men in *England*, of the same consort and faction, proceeded in effect, vpon the like occasion, for their new platforme: but yet in a different manner.

For the first ten or eleuen yeares of her Maiesties raign, through the peeuish frowardnes, the outcries and exclamations of those that came home from *Geneua*, against the garments prescribed to Ministers, and other such like matters: no man (of any experience) is ignorant, what great contention and strife was raysed: insomuch as their sectaries deuided themselues from their ordinary congregations, and meeting together in priuate houses, in woods, & fieldes, had and kept there, their disorderly and vnlawfull conuenticles.

These kinds of assemblies (notwithstanding the inconuenience and absurdnes of them in a Church reformed,) *M. Cartwright* (within a while after) tooke vppon him (in sort) to defend, saying: *that the name of conuenticles, was too light and contemptuous for them.*

T.C. 2. reply. page 38.

About the twelfth yeare of her highnesse said gouernment, these malecontents, growing weary of the foresaide dissentions, and being of restlesse dispositions, began to stir vp new quarrels, concerning the *Geneua* Discipline: being the matter indeede which they still aymed at, in all their former proceedings. Herevpon (the 14. of her Maiesty) two *admonitions* were framed, and exhibited to the high Court of Parliament. The first contayned their pretended griefes, with a declaration (forsooth) of the onely way to reforme them: vz. by admitting of that platforme, which was there described.

This admonition, finding small entertainement, (the authors or chief preferrers thereof being imprisoned) out commeth the second *admonition*, towardes the end of the same Parliament: with great lightning and thunder, as though heauen and earth shoulde haue met together, because of the little regard which was had before, to the former *admonition*. In this second *admonition*, the first is wholly iustified: the Parliament (as it hath beene shewed) is mightily challenged: great wordes are vsed, and in plaine tearmes, it is there affirmed: That if they of that assembly woulde not then followe the aduise of the first *admonition*, they would surely themselues be their owne caruers. *The Church* (say they) *may and must keepe God his orders: and surely this is only God his order*, (vz. the sayd platforme) *& ought*

2. Admonition. pa. 60. 61.

to

to bee vsed in his Church, so that in conscience wee are forced to speake for it, and to vse it.

Whereupon, presently after the sayd Parliament, (vz. the twentieth of Nouember, 1572.) there was a Presbytery erected at *Wandesworth in Surrey* (as it appeareth by a bill endorsed with *Master Fields* hande, thus: *the order of Wandesworth.*) In which order the Elders names, eleuen of them, are set downe: the manner of their election is declared: the approuers of them, (one *Smith of Micham*, and *Crane of Roughampton*) are mentioned: their offices and certaine generall rules, (then giuen vnto them to bee obserued) were likewise agreed vpon, and described.

CHAP. II.

The secrete meetinges for Discipline, and the matters handled in them here in England from 1572 till 1583.

HOwe they grew to be so farre gone at *Wandesworth*, that I find not: they of *London*, at that time, were nothing so forward. And yet, as it appeareth by the lawfull deposition and othe of one, (then of that faction, but now a very honest man, a Batcheller of Diuinity, and an auncient Preacher) they had then their meetings of Ministers, tearmed brethren, in priuate houses in *London*: as namely of *Field, Wilcox, Standen, Iackson, Bonham, Seinctloe, Crane,* and *Edmondes,* which meetinges were called conferences, according to the plot in the first and second *admonitions* mentioned.

Tho.Ed. both before the Commiss, and in the Starre Chamber.

In these *London*-meetings, at the first, *little was debated, but against subscription, the attyre, and booke of common prayer. Marry after* (saith he) *that Charke, Trauers, Barber, Gardiner,*

 Cheston,

Cheston, and lastly Crooke and Egerton, ioyned themselues into that brotherhood, then the handling of the Discipline began to be rife: then many motions were made, and conclusions were set downe. As for example.

That forasmuch, as diuers bookes had beene written, and sundry petitions exhibited to her Maiesty, the Parliament, their LL[s], *and yet to little purpose: therefore euery man, should labour, by all the meanes he could, to bring into the Church, the said reformation themselues.*

That the present gouernement of the Church, by Archbishops & Bishops, was Antichristian: & that the only Discipline & gouernment of Christ, (as they termed it,) vz. by Pastors, Doctors, Elders, and Deacons, should be established in place of the other.

That for the better bringing in of the said forme of Discipline, they should not onely, (aswell publikely as priuately) teach it, but by little and little, as much as possibly they might, draw the same into practise, though they concealed the names, either of Presbytery, Elder, or Deacon, making little account of the name for the time, so that their offices might be secretly established.

There was *an assembly of three-score Ministers, appointed out of Essex, Cambridge-shiere, and Norfolke, to meete the eighth of May, 1582. at Cockefield, (Maister Knewstubs towne) there to conferre of the common booke, what might be tollerated, & what necessarily to be refused in euery point of it: apparel, matter, forme, dayes, fastings, iniunctions, &c.*

Pig. to Field. 16. of May, 1582.

Of this meeting it is thus reported. *Our meeting was appointed to be kept very secretely, and to be made knowne to none, &c.* That this assembly was also kept accordingly, it appeareth by these words. *Concerning the meeting, I hope all things were so proceeded in, as your self would like of: aswell for reuerence to other brethren, as for other matters. I suppose before this time, some of the company, haue told you by word: for that was permitted vnto you.*

Ano.

Another meeting was also appointed to be helde, that yeare, at the *Commencement* in *Cambridge*, as is plaine by these wordes. *Concerning the Commencement, I like well your motion: desiring it might so come to passe: and that it be procured, to be as generall as might be: which may easily be brought to passe, if you at London, shall so thinke well of it, and we here may vnderstand your minde: we will (I trust) as we can, further it. M. Allen liketh well of the matter.* Pig. to Field. ibid.

Chap. III.

A forme or booke of Discipline is drawen, and a resolution is agreed vpon, how far they might proceede for the practise of it, without breaking the peace of our Church.

Hilest the brethren in the Countrey, were comming thus fast on forward (as you haue heard in the ende of the former Chapter:) you must not thinke that the *Rabbies* in *London* were in the meane time idle. Hitherto it should seeme, that in all their former proceedings, they had relied chiefly, vpon the *first admonition* and *Cartwrights* booke: as hauing had no particular and seuerall platforme, that was generally allowed of amongst them, for the Church of *England*. But now at the length, (about the yeare, 1583.) the *forme of Discipline* (which is lately come to light) was compiled: and thereupon an assembly or Councell being helde (as I thinke at *London*, or at *Cambridge*) certaine decrees were made, concerning the establishing and the practise thereof. In which decrees, mention is made of a collection, concluded vppon for the *Scottish* Ministers, fugitiues here in *England*, 1583. (which sheweth the time when they were made:) & order is likewise taken for the putting in vse of the *Synodicall Discipline*; which also prooueth the age of that booke.

The decrees themselues are extant to bee seene, vnder Maister *Wights* hande; a man of that brotherhood. But it may not be omitted, that you must thinke; how the godly brethren in all these and such other their zealous courses, had neuer any meaning to disturbe the present state established. And thereupon (forsooth) in this conspiracy or councell mentioned, (like good and quiet spirited men) they had an especiall care, that the peace of the *Church* might not be broken, by any order or decree of theirs. So as then the question amongst them was, (seeing the Discipline must needs vp) how farre they might proceede in the establishing and practise of it, keeping notwithstanding the peace of the *Church*, established already by her Maiesty. And it was ouerruled accordingly, as it followeth in the decrees themselues, faithfully translated, worde for word, out of their owne Latin coppy.

The title thereof, vz.

These be the thinges, that (doo seeme) may well stande with the peace of the Church.

The Decrees.

Let no man (though he be an Vniuersity *man) offer himself to the Ministery, nor let any man take vpon him an vncertaine and vague Ministery, though it be offered vnto him. But such as bee called to the Ministery by some certaine Church, let them impart it vnto that* Classis *or* conference, *(whereof themselues are,) or else vnto some greater* Church assembly: *and if such shall be found fit by them, then let them bee commended, by their letters vnto the* Bishop, *that they may bee ordayned Ministers by him.*

Those ceremonies in the Booke of common prayer, *which being taken from Popery, are in controuersie, doo seeme, that they ought*

ought to bee omitted and giuen ouer, if it may bee done without danger, of being put from the Ministery. But if there be any imminent danger to be depriued, then this matter must bee communicated with the Classis: in which that Church is: that by the iudgement thereof, it may be determined, what ought to be done.

If subscription to the articles of Religion, and to the booke of common Prayer, shall be againe vrged: it is thought, that the booke of articles, may be subscribed vnto, according to the statute 13. Eliz. that is, vnto such of them onely, as containe the summe of Christian faith, and doctrine of the Sacraments. But for many waighty causes, neither the rest of the articles in that booke, nor the booke of common prayer, may be allowed: no, though a man should be depriued of his Ministery for it.

It seemeth, that Churchwardens and Collectors for the poore, might thus be turned into Elders and into Deacons.

When they are to be chosen, let the Church haue warning fifteene dayes before, of the time of election, and of the ordinance of the Realme: but especially of Christs ordinance, touching appointing of watchmen and ouerseers in his Church: who are to foresee, that none offence or scandall doo arise in the Church: and if any shall happen, that by them it may be duely abolished.

And touching Deacons of both sorts (vz. men and women) the Church shall be monished, what is required by the Apostle: and that they are not to choose men, of custome and of course, or for their riches, but for their faith, zeale, and integrity: and that the Church is to pray, (in the meane time) to be so directed, that they make choise, of men that be meete.

Let the names of such as are so chosen, be published, the next Lords day: and after that, their dueties to the Church, and the Churches towards them, shall be declared: then let them be receiued vnto the Ministery, to which they are chosen, with the generall prayers of the whole Church.

The Brethren are to be requested, to ordaine a distribution of

all

all Churches, according to these rules, (in that behalfe) that are set downe in the Sinodicall Discipline, *touching* Classicall, Prouinciall, Comitiall *or of* Commencements, *and* assemblies for the whole kingdome.

The Classes *are to be required, to kepe acts of memorable matters: which they shall see deliuered to the* Comitiall assembly *that frō thence they may be broght by the* prouincial assembly.

Also, they are to deale earnestly with patrones, to present fit men: whensoeuer any Church is fallen voide in that Classis.

The Comitiall assemblies *are to bee monished, to make collections for reliefe of the poore and of schollers: but especially for reliefe of such Ministers here, as are put out, for not subscribing to the Articles, tendred by the Bishoppes: also for reliefe of* Scottish *Ministers and others, and for other profitable and necessary vses.*

All the prouinciall Synodes, *must continually, afore hand, foresee in due time, to appoint the keeping of their next* prouinciall Synodes: *and for the sending of chosen persons, with certaine instructions, vnto the* Nationall Synode *to be holden: whensoeuer the* Parliament *for the kingdome shall be called, and at some certaine set time euere yeare.*

Hitherto the *Decrees* of this graue *Councell*, whereby it seemeth to me, that when they resolued, they might proceede thus farre, and keepe (notwithstanding) the peace of the Church of *England* established: they opposed (in that resolution) the worde *peace*, to *warre:* as though they should haue agreed, how far they might runne on in this race, without vrging of their followers, to force & armes. For otherwise, how could any sober men, so much as once haue imagined, that they might, in this sort, ouerthrow (in effect) the present gouernement, and establish their owne deuises, and yet neuer breake the peace of the Church? But I will not presse this point. It is more agreeable to my purpose to pursue the chase.

Chap.

CHAP. IIII.

About the yeare, 1583. they fell againe to the practise of their Discipline, and of a Consistorian question.

TO make good lawes, and not see them executed, is but labour lost. And therefore it should seeme, that these wise *Law-makers*, were presently after, as carefull to put the sayde orders in practise, as they were before to resolue vpon them: as it may appeare by a letter, written to Master *Field* from *Antwerpe*, the 25. of *Iune*, 1583. by one *Cholmeley*, in answere of a former Letter, sent vnto him from the said *Field*. For thus *Cholmeley* writeth: *Lætor intùs & in corde, de meliori successu rerum vestrarum, quòd cum de conuentibus vestris audiam, tum de Disciplinæ Ecclesiasticæ formali πράξει multò lubentissimè. Dicam quòd verum est, serò nimis incepistis: quisquis iam tandem vel incipere recusauerit, vel a tam præclaro incepto desistat, peccatum suum feret: pænitendum est de priori lentitudine. I am glad with all my heart, for the better successe of your affaires, not onely in that I heare of your assemblies, but most willingly of all, in respect of your effectuall practising of the Ecclesiasticall Discipline. I will tell you that which is true, you haue begun this course too too late. Whosoeuer shall now, either refuse to begin, or shall desist from so notable an enterprise, he shall beare his owne sin. You ought to repent you for your former slownes.* And afterward, thus out of the same Letter, to incourage Maister *Field* and the brethren. *In nulla re terreamini ab ijs qui se opponunt, quod illis quidem est exitij indicium, vobis autem salutis, idque a Deo. In nothing feare your aduersaries, which is to them a token of perdition, but to you of saluation, and that from God.* Philip. 1.

In *Iuly* the next yeare, vz. 1584. some of the *Scottish* Mi- Gelbrand to Field.

 nisters

nisters afore spoken of, went to *the Act in Oxford:* where Maister *Gelibrand* with his brethren, gaue them *great entertainement*. At that time, there was a notable question propounded amongst their fauourers there, by the sayde Ministers, as is manifest by these wordes. *Here haue beene a good company of godly brethren this Act.* Maister Fen, Wilcox, Axton: *the Scottish ministers, and wee haue had some meeting and conference, to our great comfort that are here. One point* (which then was moued) *I would wish to be throughly debated among you and them, concerning the proceeding of the Minister in his duety, without the assistance or tarrying for the Magistrate, &c.*

What was resolued amongst the brethren of *London*, about this matter at that time, I know not. Marry this I finde, that presently thereupon, they grewe more violent, and prepared themselues to proceede more resolutely, in the challenging of their Discipline, as it is plaine by the dealing both of them, and of their fauourers, that yeare in *Nouember* and *December* after, at the *Parliament*, 27. of her Maiesty.

And besides, let the sayd Maister *Gelibrands* words, in a Letter to *Field*, dated the 12. of *Ianuary* after, vz. 1584. bee considered. For (as it seemeth to me) they either tend to sedition, or to the admitting, in *Oxford*, of the foresayd *Decrees* or *Discipline*. Sure I am, that they can hardly (for ought I see) receiue any good construction. Thus he writeth

I haue already entred into the matters, whereof you write, and dealt with three or foure of seuerall Colleges, *concerning those among whom they liue. I finde, that men are very dangerous in this point, generally fauoring reformation: but when it commeth to the particular point, some haue not yet considered of these things, for which others in the Church are so much troubled: others*

thers are afraid to testifie any thing with their hands, least it breed danger before the time. And after: *many fauour the cause of reformation, but they are not Ministers, but young students, of whome there is good hope, if it be not cut off by violent dealing before the time. As I heare by you, so I meane to goe forward, where there is any hope, and to learne the number, and to certifie you thereof.*

Furthermore, at the time of the *Parliament* last mentioned, I finde, that there was a *nationall Synode* helde likewise in *London* by these brethren: according to their former decisions and *Synodicall* Discipline. This appeareth by three letters. The first was, from *eleuen ministers of Essex*, to *Field:* 26. Ia. 1584.
wherin they desire to *be certified, whether the brethren meant to be exercised, in prayer and fasting, and vpon what day*. The seconde was, from *nine of the saide* Ministers, to Fielde and Charke: wherein they writ thus: *We haue elected two Godly* 2. Febru. 1584.
and faithfull brethren, Maister Wright and Maister Gifford, to ioyne with you in that businesse. The third was, from *Gelibrand, to Field:* 29. Nouemb. 1584.
Wherein he excuseth himselfe of a great ouersight, in these words. *Touching my departure from that holy assembly without leaue, &c. I craue pardon, both of you & them, &c. And thus* (sayth he) *commending this holy cause to the Lord himselfe, and your godly counsaile to the President thereof, I take my leaue.*

Chap. V.

Their Booke of Discipline is reuiewed: it was after sent abroad about, 1587. it was put in practise, in Northamptonshire and many other places.

Notwithstanding that the booke of Discipline was abroad, as it hath beene noted, (in the third chapter,) and that the brethren had framed themselues (as they might) vnto the rules thereof: yet there were found, some imperfections in it: which in the *Synode*, mentioned in the former chapter, (as I take it) were referred to Maister *Trauers*, to bee corrected and ordered by him, as his leysure will permitte. Which appeareth by a letter of Maister *Fields* to Maister *Trauers*, in these words. *Concerning our other busines: I would wish, that the Discipline were read ouer with as much speed as could be, and that some good directions were giuen, for the brethren abroad, who are earnest to enter some good course, for the furtherance of the L: cause.* And after in the same place: *I finde many abroade, very willing to ioyne with the best: to put in practise that which shall bee agreed vpon, by the brethren. If it might please the brethren therefore, that those or the like instructions (which wee had) with a perfect coppie of the Discipline, might be sent, I would wholly imploy my selfe in that seruice.* Another also vpon the longer stay thereof. *I pray you hasten the forme of Discipline and send it.* And the same man againe: *I pray you remember the forme of Discipline, which Master Trauers promised to make perfect, and send it me when it is finished. We will put it in practise, and trie mens minds therein, as we may.*

Field to Trauers. 3. Iulie. 1585.

Gelibrand to Field. 9. of Nouem. 1585

Gelibrand to Field, 30. Ianuarie.

According to these requests, the draught of Discipline was at the last finished: and then sent abroade, to be approued generally by all the brotherhood, as may thus appear: *The discipline we haue receiued, and we giue you and the brethren hartie thanks for it. As yet we are not resolued in all points of it: hauing had but small time to peruse it, nor the commoditie of often meeting about it. But we haue taken order for our monthly assembly, and after our owne consents yeelded vnto it, for associating other into our companie, whom we shall thinke approued.* And an other. *We hartilie giue God thanks* (sayth one) *for the godly & most Christian paines of the brethren, in the trauaile of the Discipline: which is come to our hands to be considered-of Gelibrands* letter of his receit of the booke of Discipline, was written

Gelibrand to Field.

Sandes to Field 20. Iune 1587.

in

in the name of the brethren in *Oxford*. At which time there was another Synode held in *London: whither* (sayth the letter) *Maister West and Maister Browne were sent from Oxford: to whom they referred the estate of their Church, to be related: and by whom they desired to vnderstand, directions from the Synode, how they might deale afterwardes in those matters.*

Within a while after, vz. 1587. (as I suppose,) there was in like sort an *assemblie or Synode helde of the Cambridgeshire brotherhood:* accompanied peraduenture with some of other shires. About which time also, vpon the new edition of the foresayd booke, the further practise of the *Discipline* mentioned by *Cholmeley, 1583.* (as is before shewed) began to spread it selfe more freely, into the most parts of the *Realme:* but especially (for ought I doo yet vnderstand) it was most friendly intertained, amongst the ministers of *Northamptonshire*, as it appeareth in recorde by some of their owne depositions, 16. of May, 1590. in these wordes following. *About two yeares and a halfe, since the whole shire was diuided into three Classes. 1. The Classis of Northamptonshire, consisting of these Ministers: Maister Snape, Maister Penrie, Maister Sibthorpe, Maister Edwards, Maister Littleton, Maister Bradshaw, Maister Larke, Maister Fleshware, Maister Spicer, &c. 2. The Classis of Dauentrie side, consisting of these: Maister Barebon, Maister Rogers, Maister King, Maister Smart, Maister Sharpe, Maister Prowdloe, Maister Elliston, &c. 3. The Classis of* Kettring *side: consisting of these: Master Stone, Maister Williamson, Maister Fawsbrooke, Maister Patinson, Maister Massey &c.*

This appeareth vnder M. Wights hand.

M. Iohnson. So in effect M. Litleton M. Sharpe.

This deuise (saith *Maister Iohnson*) *is commonly receiued in* most [a] *parts of England, (as I haue heard in sundrie of our meetings:) but especially, in* Warwickshire, Suffolke, Norfolke, Essex, &c.

a *M.* Snape reported as much, as Edward Smith, Ri. Hawgar & Ri. Holme haue deposed

The

b M Sharpe and M. Litleton doe likewise herein agree with M. Iohnson.

The maner of euery perticular Classis is this. At [b] their meeting (which is alwaies in some priuate house, but yet in their Mother Cities) first a moderator is chosen, in this sort: One of them conceiueth a praier, for Gods direction in that choyse.

Then he, that conceiued the praier, sitteth alone in scrutonie: and euery one giueth his voice secretlie vnto him. He that hath most voyces is chosen.

The moderator, thus chosen, conceiueth another praier: that God would blesse him in the course of his office. Then being set at the tables end, with his brethren by him: the names of all the brethren are called. If any were absent at their first sitting downe, he sitteth after in order, as he commeth, for auoiding of superioritie.

The authoritie of the moderator endureth vntill the next meeting of that Classis. At the breaking vp of euery Classis, there is euer some certaine time appointed, when they shall meete againe: which is sometime within a fortnight, but commonly three weeks at the furthest: If any thing do fall out in the meane time, fit to be consulted vpon: the moderator may call the Classis together sooner, according to an order made amongst themselues.

a Mast. Litleton deposeth as much.

It is [a] a generall order, that when any is admitted into a Classis: he doth promise vnder his hand, that he will submit himselfe, and be obedient to all such orders and decrees, as shall be set down by the same Classis to be obserued.

As for example: these were part of the particular articles, whereunto euerie one of Northampton Classis did subscribe, at his entring or admittance into it: we doo promise to submit our selues, vnto such orders and decrees, as shall be set downe by our Classis: We do promise to submit our selues, to be censured by our brethren of this Classis, in all matters concerning doctrine and Discipline, &c.

In this Classis it was furthermore concluded and agreed vpon, that when any controuersie did arise, touching any matters of doctrine, or about the interpretation of any place of Scriptures: euerie

uerie one of that Classis, should alwaies yeeld therein, vnto that interpretation and resolution, which the brethren of that Classis should determine of. And so also when any questions did rise amongest them of greater difficultie. As for example, Maister Stone mooued this question to the Northampton Classis in the behalfe of one: vz. two are contracted: one of them marrieth with a third: hee or shee so married, are free againe; The question is; whether the former contract, doo nowe againe binde. And the resolution was: it did not: which was a false Resolution.

The determinations and acts concluded vpon in this Classis, were registred in a booke by Snape: chosen Register by the companie, and who alwaies kept the same.

Mast. Sharpe to the same purpose of Dauentry Classis.

Besides these perticular Classes, there is another kind of meeting, which is termed the Assembly. And it consisteth (for example) in Northamptonshire, of the number of six: that is two of euery Classis, which are sent thither by election. The ordinarie place of this assembly in Northãptonshire, was at Northampton: where Snape commonly was one, and a chiefe man, Barbon & King, were the men that vsually came from Dauentry side: and Stone and Williamson from Kettring side.

At the meeting of the sixe, there is alwaies a moderator first chosen, in manner and forme, as in the Classis: and so likewise for their further order of proceeding. The moderator continueth his authoritie, ouer all the three Classes, vntill the like meeting happen again: which is neuer certain. But yet commonly within six or eight weeks, vpon occasion signified from the Classes vnto this moderator. For vnto him belongeth the calling of this assembly.

The matters, which here are handled, are those of great moment; such as concerne the state of the Church generally. As for example: the writing of letters to the brethren at Oxford, Cambridge, & London: to certifie them of their proceedings, & to know what course is held amongst them, in those places, for the

The like Ma. Sharpe of Dauentry Classis

the Discipline and gouernement, which they tearme Reformation:) *to the intent, that the particular* Classes, *vpon their aduertisements, may direct themselues, and their Churches accordingly.*

It is likewise alwaies concluded, at such times, which of the sixe assembled, shall penne the letters. And in this choise, Snape *was commonly the man.*

The men, to whom they vsuallie did write: were one in Cambridge; Trauers *in* London, *and* Gelibrand *in* Oxford: *When any answeres were returned from those places: they were commonly directed to* Snape, *or to him that had written to them, in the name of the brethren.*

M. Sharpe to to the same purpose of Dauentrie Classis.

Two especiall points (I remember) were concluded in this assemblie: the one was, for a suruay of all the Churches in Northhamptonshire: *th'other, for an order to bee obserued at the last* Parliament, *which then drew neere.*

The suruay was, to know what euerie benefice in the shire was worth, how many soules by a generall coniecture, were in euerie parish: who were the incumbents, and of what life, paines and qualities they were. To this purpose, the fittest men, and such as were best acquainted in the shire were nominated: as Litleton *for* Haddon *Deanerie, &c. Which dutie he performed for his part to the vttermost: and brought a most rayling Discourse, against euery Minister, which was not of our companie.*

The end propounded of this suruey, was: vz. that if vpon signification to the brethren abroad, what was done there: they would likewise make the like suruey in other countries: the Parliament *(if neede required, and to the better furthering of their purposes) might haue a generall viewe, of all the Ministers in* England, *that impugned their desires.*

The second point before mentioned was this: vz. a conclusion to send vp to London, *one or two of euerie* Classis *in* Northhamptonshire, *with letters of credite, to attend at the* Parliament:

ment: *to ioine themselues with the brethren of other countries: and to offer disputation, (if it should be so thought meete) and to vndertake any other such matter, as should then and there be determined of amongst them: and that there should be letters written, of this resolution, to know how the brethren abroad liked it: or what other course they would hold, at that time, for the bringing in of Discipline and Church gouernement.*

These two points, were penned by Snape: *and sent to the brethren abroad, as it was ordered.*

What answere was returned to Snape, *from the brethren in* Oxford *&* Cambridge, *I know not: but well I remember, that* Trauerse *did write to* Snape, *a very cunning Letter: wherein he shewed himselfe not to mislike the foresaid suruay to be generallie made, but signified, that the Parliament drawing on so fast, it could not be done so soone. But for the second point: that (he writ) was liked, and meete to be followed.*

Whereupon the Classes *of* Northamptonshire, *did send vp some three or fower, as* Settle *for* Northampton, Rogers *for* Dauentry, *&c. with a further conclusion, that if any of them (vpon occasion) should be committed, others should be sent vp in their places.*

Although the time was short, for the generall accomplishing of these forenamed pointes: yet this examinate thinketh, some thing was done in the first: vz. as hee hath heard, a suruay was made to the purpose before touched, of the Ministers in North-folke, Suffolke *and* Essex. *And for the second, true it was, that many were sent to attend at the* Parliament, *from the most parts of England. And one resolution was, that some twenty or thirty of them, should haue come in their gownes, with all grauitie, to the* Parliament-*house-dore; and there haue desired by petition a disputation.*

This suruey hath beene made in the most shires of England: as by the surueies themselues to be shewed it appeareth. They are in maner of heathnish libels.

Furthermore, concerning some censures vsed, there was a generall consent and purpose, amongest the brethren, touching a se-

cret kinde of excommunication: for examples sake. A lay man committeth some sinne. One of the Elders was to admonish him. The partie is obstinate. The Elder must take two or three with him the second time. And if this serue not, then he is to be debarred from the communion. In this case, if the said party should (notwithstanding) intrude himselfe to communicate, then it was agreed to repell him, vppon pretence of certaine words in the communion booke. So as thereby, they might keepe their owne course, for their Discipline, and yet haue a cloake to couer them withall, out of the booke.

Againe, an other thing is notable to this effect. About a yeare and a halfe a goe, Iohn Nelson of Northampton, an Elder or a Deacon of Saint Peters, (as I thinke) hauing eyther his daughter, or his sister gotten with childe, in his house, by one of his seruants, Master Snape dealt with the said seruant, to vrge him to publicke repentaunce: and at the last, so farre preuailed with him, (as it was thought,) that he promised the next sunday so to doe: but came not. Whereupon Snape made a verie bitter Sermon against him. The next Sonday he came indeede. And then Snape made a long praier, that God would giue him grace, to make a faithfull acknowledgement of his sinne &c. That done, the penitentiary, made publique confession &c. Which being perfourmed, Snape absolued him; and then entred into a great discourse how cleare the partie was, and free from that sinne committed, euen as though he had bin newlie born: charging the congregation, that no man should presume, at any time after, to obiect the same vnto him. But that, which was most wondred at: whereas this poore man was thus dealt withall, Snape caused lame Prettie, a Souldier of Barwicke (who without any calling in the Church at all, sauing that he had a telleration to read, did such seruice in that place, as was appointed by Snape to bee read, till he came to Church) the next morning to marrie the saide penitentiarie to the woman with childe before named, without anie

bring-

bringing of her, vnto anie such publicke repentance. Hereof, grew amongst the people great speech, that the pore man was so vsed, & the richer mans sister or daughter was so freed. The saide lame Souldier, hath married manie in that place, vpon Snapes *commaundement: for that* Snape *holdeth, that dutie to appertaine no more to the Ministers office, then to anie other man.*

And as touching that point mentioned, of the brethe-rens submitting of themselues, by subscription, to be censured in their *Classis:* it was thus vsed in the *Northampton Classis. The brethren being together in a chamber, the partie to be first censured,* (as they were all to be in course) *goeth forth out of the chamber. Then the moderator asketh euery mans opinion of him: how he behaueth himselfe aswell in his life, as in his Ministerie: and euerie man, hauing spoken his opinion, the partie is called in: and then, if he were not any way touched, he is greatly commended: if otherwise, then reprooued, as the causes require. For example,* Edwards *of* Cortnall *comming vnder this censure, was blamed for vsing the Crosse in Baptisme: and at his comming-in againe, was wonderfull sharpely dealt withall for the same.*

Thus farre *Maister Iohnson* of the *Northampton Classis.* With whom doe allso agree in the principall points: *Maister Littleton,* as touching the same *Classis, Maister Sharpe,* & *Maister Walker, Preachers and persons deposed,* concerning the *Classis* of *Dauentry* side: and *Maister Stone* (a Preacher likewise) vpon his oth, for that of *Kettring* side. One or two points I may not omitte, which *Maister Stone* hath deliuered. He confesseth *that at diuers times, Maister* Snape, *Maister* Barbon; *Maister* Sharpe, *Maister* Prowdloe, *Maister* King, *Maister* Iohnson, *Maister* Sibthorp, *Maister* Spicer, *Maister* Baxter, *Maister* Littleton, *Maister* Williamson, *Maister* Bradshaw, *Maister* Fleshware, *Maister* Harrison, *and hee, haue mette in* Northampton : *and likewise at*

Stone in the Starchamber.

Kettring: *and at his house, the most of them, with some others as Maister* Rishbrooke, *Maister* Atkinson, *Maister* Dauyes, *Maister* Massye, *Maister* Okes *&c. about matters of discipline.* And he saith further, *that in an assembly had, either at his house or at* Kettring, *it was propounded, treated, and concluded, that the Apocrypha writings were not to be read in the Church. And* in an other assembly, which of them he doth not remember, he affirmeth likewise, *that it was debated and concluded vpon, that the superiority of the Bishops of this land, ouer the rest of the Ministers, is not warranted by the word of God.*

To these depositions, concerning the *Northamptonshire Classes*, I might adde the depositions of one maister *Parker*, Vicar of *Dedham* in *Essex*, for the proofe of the *Classes* in that shire: as of one about *Brayntree side*, consisting of these Ministers, maister *Culuerwell*, maister *Rogers*, maister *Gifford &c.* another about *Colchester*, consisting of these Ministers, Doctor *Chapman*, Doctor *Chricke*, maister *Dowe*, maister *Farrar*, maister *Newman*, master *Tey* &c. and so likewise the depositions of others.

Hen. Asker to Field. Apr. 14. 1585.

Ego singulis sabbatis, si non alius aduenions locum suppleat, cum prescripta leiturgias formula nihil habens cōmertij; in cœtu concionem habeo: idque reuerendorum fratrum consilio, qui suos habent singulis ferè hebdomadis conuentus, qui etiam me in eorum numerum, (sic est mihi propitius Deus,) benigne ascripserunt. I preach euery Sabbaoth day, (if no other that commeth by chance, doth supply the place) hauing nothing to do at all with the forme or booke of Common Prayer: and that by the counsell of the reuerend brethren: who haue their meetinges almost euery weeke, who haue also, (God being so mercifull vnto me) admitted me very kindly into their number.

But in following of that course, I should be too tedious. I will onely set downe, one mans witnesse more, agreeing with Master *Iohnson*, for the proofe, that the like *Classes*, are or haue beene held in most Shires in England: and so referring you to iudge of them all, by that of *Northampton*, I will goe forward.

About two yeares since, Maister *Snape* did say and affirme, in the presence of *Edward Smith, Robert Vicars, Edward Birde, Richard Holmes, & himselfe, that there were three or foure small* Classes *of Ministers in euery shire, where there were any learned Preachers, who did vse (in their meetinges) to debate of the Discipline, by Pastors, Doctors, Elders, & Deacons, and that the said seuerall small* Classes, *did send their resolutions and opinions, to the greater assemblies at* Cambridge *at* Sturbridge *Fayre time, and at* London *at* Bartholomew *Fayre time, which did meete together also for the same purpose: and that if the said great* assembly *did like of that, which was done by the smaller* Classes, *then was the same (so liked of) generally concluded, to be that, which ought to be, or stand, in the Church.* (As for example.) *That it was concluded and agreed vpon, both in the said* Classicall *and* generall assemblies; *that the dumbe ministerie was no ministerie, or else no lawfull ministerie: and that the Ministers in their seuerall charges, should all teach one kind of doctrine, tending to the erecting of the foresaid gouernement, by* Pastors, Doctors, Elders *and* Deacons: *which pointes (sayth Holmes* of himselfe in another examination) *were concluded in the Synode at* Sturbridge *Fayre last. vz. 1588.*

Chap. VI.

A Synode is held at Couentrie, 1588. many questions are resolued, the booke of Discipline is subscribed vnto.

THere is mention made, in the last chapter, of a Synode or meeting, 1587. of the *Cambridgeshire Classicall* Ministers, and peraduenture of some others also with them. In which meeting there were certain que-

 stions

stions propounded & dealt in: the which questions were afterwards sent by their direction, to the *Warwickshire Classes*, or brethren assembled in those parts, to bee further intreated of and resolued.

The next yeare after, vz. 1588. the saide *Warwickeshire Classes, &c.* assembling themselues together, in councel, (as it seemeth at *Couentry*,) the questions mentioned, were determined vpon: and besides, other matters were also concluded, as by the acts themselues following (to be shewed vnder *Maister Wights* hand, and are acknowledged in effect vppon two mens othes in the *Starre-chamber*) may sufficiently appeare. Thus the proceedinges of that meeting are intituled. *Acta conuentus Classium Warwic, die decimo, quarti. 1588. The Acts of the assembly of the Warwickeshire Classes the tenth day of the fourth moneth.* And touching the questions specified. *Questiones a fratribus ex Synodo Cantabrigiensi, anno superiore delatæ, eâ quæ sequitur formulâ sunt explicatæ. The questions brought the other yeare, from the brethren of the* Cambridge Synode, *are resolued in manner as followeth.* I will not trouble my paper with the fourme which they vsed, but these were some of their resolutions: vz.

That priuate Baptisme is vnlawfull.

That it is not lawfull, to read homilies in the Church.

That the signe of the Crosse, is not to be vsed in Baptisme.

That the faithfull ought not to communicate with vnlearned ministers, although they may be present at their seruice, if they come of purpose to heare a sermon. The reason is, because lay men, aswell as ministers, may read publike seruice.

That the calling of Bishops &c. is vnlawfull.

That as they deale in causes ecclesiasticall, there is no duety belonging vnto them, nor any, publikely to be giuen them.

That it is not lawful, to be ordained by thē into the ministery, or to denounce either suspensions or excommunications sent from thē.

That

That it is not lawfull, to rest in the Bishops depriuation of any from the ministerie, except (vpon consultation with the neighbor-ministers adioyning, and his flocke) it seeme so good vnto them: but that he continue in the same, vntill he be compelled to the contrary by ciuill force.

That it is not lawfull, to appeare in a Bishops Court: but with protestation of their vnlawfulnes.

That Bishops are not to be acknowledged, either for Doctors, Elders, *or* Deacons, *as hauing no ordinary calling.*

That touching the restauration of their Ecclesiasticall discipline, it ought to be taught to the people, data occasione, *as occasion should serue.*

That nondum *(as yet) the people are not to be solicited,* publicè *(publickly) to the practise of the discipline:* donec, *(till) they be better instructed in the knowledge of it.*

That men of better vnderstanding, are to be allured priuatly, to the present imbracing of the Discipline and practise of it, as far as they shall be well able, with the peace of the Church. And thus farre the *prouinciall Synode* of the *Warwickeshire Classis.*

Likewise at that time, there was in the same assembly, a great approbation obtained of the foresaid booke of *Discipline*, as to be a *draught of Discipline, essentiall & necessarie for all times*: and certaine articles (being deuised in approbation, and for the maner of the vse of that booke,) were then brought forth, treated-of, and subscribed vnto, (as Maister *Nutter* & Maister *Cleuely*, two that were then present, haue deposed,) *by* Maister *Cartwright*, Maister *Fenne*, Maister *Wight, &c. who promised to guide themselues by the saide Discipline, and according to it, as it is set downe in the saide articles,* which herafter shall be likewise declared. It appeareth also by the said parties depositions, that diuers others did subscribe at the same time, (or at the least within a short time after,) but they might not (forsooth) by reason of their

Nutter and Cleueley in the Starre-chamber

owne

owne consciences, name them. Howbeit the matter is otherwise plaine inough, who they were: by a note taken with *Maister Litleton: vz. Iohn Oxenbridge, Edward Gellibrand, Hercules Cleuely, Anthony Nutter, Leonard Fetherstone, Mathew Hulme, Edward Lord, &c.*

This booke, hauing thus at the last receaued this great allowance, more authentically: was carried farre and nere, for a generall ratification of all the brethren. It was offered to the *Dauentry side* Classis, as *Master Sharp and Master Walker* haue deposed; and likewise at *Northampton by Penry*, as *Maister Litleton* affirmeth. But that, which *Maister Iohnson* hath set downe, is worthy the remembrance. The effect of it, is this: *that when the booke of Discipline came to Northampton, to be subscribed vnto: there was a generall censuring vsed amongst the brethren there, as it were to sanctifie themselues, partly by sustaining a kinde of penance, and reproofe for their former conformity, to the orders of the Church, established by her Maiestie, and other matters of conuersation: and partly to prepare their mindes for the deuout accepting of the foresaid booke.* In which course of censuring vsed at that time, there was such ripping vp, one of anothers life, euen from their youth, as that they came vnto great bitternes, with many *reuiling tearms* amongst themselues, one growing thereby odious to another, and some did *thereupon vtterly forsake those kinde of assemblies.*

Sharpe and Walker before the Commissioners.

Iohnson before the Commissioners.

Chap. VII.

The booke of the pretended Discipline is made perfect at Cambridge: certaine Synodes are kept: and of their estimation.

IT might haue beene deemed, that after so many viewes, *Synodes*, and subscriptions, this worthy draught of discipline, would haue growne to great

great perfection: but it falleth out otherwise. For (as it is confessed vppon othe) at *Sturbridge Fayre*-time, the next yeare (after the sayd *Classicall* counsell of the *Warwicke-shire* brethren) vz. in the yeare, 1589. there was another *Synode* or generall meeting, helde *in Saint Iohns Colledge in Cambridge. Where* (saith M. Barber) *they did correct, alter, and amend diuers imperfections conteined in the booke, called* Disciplina ecclesiæ sacra, verbo Dei descripta: *and* (as maister *Stone* affirmeth) *did not onely perfect the saide forme of Discipline, but also did then and there, (as he remembreth,) voluntarily agree amongst themselues, that so many as would should subscribe to the saide booke of Discipline after that time.* The persons, that met in this assembly, were as these two last deponents affirme,) *maister Cartwright, maister Snape, maister Allen, maister Gifford, maister Perkins, maister Stone, maister Barber, maister Harrison, with others, &c.*

I finde mention also of another Synode, 1589. held (as I take it) at *Ipswich*. Thus one *Iohn Warde* did write, that yeare, to certaine at *Ipswich: I thinke not to come ouer, till the Synode, which is (as I take it) a moneth after* Michaelmas.

It hath beene obserued before, out of maister *Edmonds* deposition: cap. 2. who were the *Classicall* brethren of *London*. It is also fit to be vnderstood, who they are, that most commonly met there also, at their more *generall, prouinciall* or *nationall* assemblies or Synodes. And this both *maister Barber*, and *maister Stone*, doo sufficiently declare. *For the space of about foure yeares last past*, (saith maister Barber,) *and since the last Parliament*, (saith maister Stone,) *there haue bin seuerall meetings in* London, *at the houses of maister Gardiner, maister Egerton, maister Trauers, and maister Barber. The persons, that vsually mette in these assemblies,* (saith maister Barber,) *were maister Cartwright, maister Charke, maister Trauers, maister Egerton, maister Gardiner, maister Oxenbridge, maister Gelibrand, maister Culuerwell, maister Browne of Oxford, maister Allen, maister Gifford, maister Sommerscales, and himselfe.*

Maister Cartwright, maister Trauers, and maister Egerton, were at sundry times chosen Moderators *or* Presidents *in the said assemblies.* And afterwardes generally of the office of the *Moderators. The resolutions, conclusions, and determinations of such matters, as were disputed of, and agreed-vpon, by the more number of them, that so disputed in the said assemblies: were by the saide* Moderators or Presidents, *before named, at the times and places of the saide seuerall assemblies, summarily and briefly, either written in a booke, or otherwise set-downe in loose papers, as to the saide* Moderators, or Presidentes *should bee thought meet or conuenient.*

As the *Classicall* assemblies of *London* were of greater estimation, then those in the Country: so these more generall meetings or Synodes last mentioned, were of highest authoritie: and indeed the *grand test* of all the rest. It may be said truely of them both, that they haue been the kindling sparkes of all those flames, which are in the Church. What was there ordered, went, as perfectly currant. From thence, the brethren, of other places, did fetch their light. As doubts did arise, thither they were sent to be resolued. The *Classicall* and *Synodicall decrees* in other places, were neuer authenticall indeede, (as it seemeth,) till there they were ratified. The chiefest directions, for all the brethren else-where, were sent from thence. It is wonderfull to consider, how men so obstinate and wilfull in their owne waies against the Church of *England*, established by her Maiestie; should be brought to submit themselues in such sort, as they did, to be led by these assemblies, as elswhere it doth appeare.

CHAP.

Chap. VIII.

Vpon some detecting of the premisses some were called into question: they refuse to be examined: all they were charged, which is in effect confessed.

IN the yeare, 1590. vpon the detecting (before some of her *Maiesties Commissioners in causes Ecclesiasticall*) of the most of these things, wherof I haue hitherto spoken: *Interrogatories* were drawen, containing in them the effect of all the premisses; and diuers such Ministers were sent for, as were sayde to haue beene the chiefe ringleaders in all those actions, Accordingly they appeared: but in the place when they shuld be examined, they refused to answere vpon their othes. Diuers pretences therof were made, as one; that first theywould see the *Interrogatories*, whereof they should be examined. The generall summe of them, was imparted vnto them: and it was likewise told them, that they should bee charged to answere no further, then by the lawes of the Realme they were bound to doo. But all this would not serue. Whervpon the *Interrogatories* themselues were shewed vnto some, as namely to *Maister Snape*, who stood most at the first vppon that point, and did pretend, that if first hee might see them, hee would then aunswere vnto them. But the issue was accordingly, as it was expected: For hauing perused them, he was further-of, then he was before: and writ to his friends, what was the summe of them: to the intent they might *be forewarned*, and so (as he sayd) *become better armed.* Which course taken by him: was not without the great prouidence of God. For thereby their whole plot, and all in effect, that was laid to their charges, was discouered. His Letters were intercepted,

In the Prefac

wherein he writeth after this sort.

Snape to N.N. 1590.

Reuerend and beloued, this day Aprill the 7. I haue beene againe before the Commissioners: After much adoo, I obtained to see and peruse the Articles against mee, (but briefly and in their presence onely,) they are many, (36.37. besides those vnder mine owne hand,) and very large, some twelue, some twenty lines long, consisting of many branches. As far as I could (for the time) conceaue and remember, they may be referred to these two heads: some concerning my selfe, together with others, and some touching my selfe alone. The former sort are touching Classes *and* Synodes: *wherein there are mentioned particular places:* (London, Oxford, Cambridge:) *times* (Act, Commencement, Sturbridge fayre, Tearme:) *persons,* (Cartwright, Perkins, Trauers, Charke, Egerton, Barbon, Stone, Snape, Knewstub, Allin, Dike, *& diuers others, &c.) and some things dealt-in and agreed vpon, &c.* By all which, besides many other thinges specified, it is most euident, that they haue manifest and certaine knowledge, not onely of generals, but also of specials and particulars.

Snape to Barbon Aprill 11. 1590. and so also to Stone.

Beloued, I haue twise appeared before the high Commissioners: the first time, the issue was prison: the second, close prison. This is my state now: the causes of both, and the proceedings in both, you shall receaue of Maister Knightlye, *the former more large in a Dialogue, the latter more briefly in a Letter: both vnperfect, both vnperused: reade them, and returne them with what speede you may: for I haue now no coppy of them: let them be wisely kept, lest they breede more anger. I haue procured another coppy to be sent to Master* Stone, *that in both places you might be forewarned, & forearmed. Touching the conferences, those of our Countrey, are yet more particularly discouered: persons (besides those there named)* Kinge, *of* Coleworth: Prowdloe, *of* Weeden, *&c.* Spicer, *of* Cogenho: Edwardes, *of* Cortenhall, *&c. places:* Sharpes *house at* Fawseley: Snapes *chamber at* Northampton,

ton, *&c. Si quis coniecturæ sit locus: I would iudge* Iohn Iohnson *to haue beene the man: because (to my remembrance) persons and thinges of his time beeing mentioned, hee onely is not named. Whosoeuer and howsoeuer, wee see the Lord calleth vs to be more resolute. They will not, they cannot be any longer concealed: now whether it were better and more safe, that one man with the consent of the rest, should boldly, freely, and wisely, confesse and lay open, &c. or that some weake (or wicked) man shoulde without consent, and in euill sort acknowledge, &c. Iudge you: the thing they ayme-at, is: A conuenticle. It must come to tryall. In the cause of murther, &c. it is wont to be enquired, whether the party fled vpon it: consider and apply to this matter, and the Lord giue vs wisedome in all things. It were good you sent to* T. C. *with speede.*

CHAP. IX.

Cartwright is called for, by authority: a Synode is held in London: it is there resolued that he shall refuse to be examined vppon his othe.

AFterwarde the same yeare before mentioned, 1590. (in *September*, as I take it,) Maister *Cartwright* vpon occasion was sent for, by the sayd Commissioners. Now, *about a weeke or a fortnight before*, Cartwright *was committed*, (sayth Maister *Stone*) whereas, the question mentioned by *Snape* to *Barbon* & the brethren: (which, as it seemeth, troubled them all:) vz. *whether it were not fit, that one man with the consent of the rest, should boldly, freely, and wisely, confesse and lay open &c.* came to be disputed in London. *There was a* Synode *or meeting, held at Maister* Gardiners, *by these brethren, Maister* Cartwright, *Maister* Charke, *Maister* Trauerse, *Maister* Egerton, *Maister* Cardiner, *Maister* Barbon, *Maister* Barber, Depos. in the Star-chamber.

maister Oxenbridge, *maister* Gelibrand, *master* Culuerwel, *my selfe, and certaine other Ministers: and they did then and there debate and consider amongst themselues, whether it were fit or conuenient, that the said maister* Cartwright, (*after his commitment to prison*) *should discouer or reueale, all or any the matters, which passed in conference and disputation, in any of their former assemblies, or not.* What the resolution hereof was, whether through the examiners ouersight, or Maister *Stones* peruersenesse, (I know not) but it is not set downe. Howbeit the effects which followed, do make it manifest.

For maister *Cartwright*, about the time before limited, being conuented: and moued in the Consistory at *Paules*, by the *Bishop* of *London*, the then two *Lordes chiefe Iustices*, maister Iustice *Gawdy*, maister *Sergeant Puckering, now Lord Keeper of the great Seale of England*, maister *Attorney Generall, now Lorde Chiefe Iustice of England*: and diuers others her Maiesties Commissioners then present to take his oth to answere to certaine *Interrogatories*: yet notwithstanding that the chiefe points of them were then deliuered in generall tearmes vnto him, & that the said both honourable and graue persons, did (euery man) seuerally assure him vpon their credits, that by the lawes of the Realme he was bound to take his oath, & therevpon to answere, as he was required: he desired to be borne withall, and said that hee thought he was not bound by the lawes of God so to do.

Chap. X.

Further proofe for their practise of their Discipline: collected out of the rules of their subscribed booke.

IF hitherto, as yet the point (I haue in hand) be not sufficiently prooued: vz. that our *English reformers* haue attempted after the *Scottish* Ministers fashion, to bring into the Church of *England*, their pretended *Disci-*

Disciplinarian gouernement, of themselues, and by their owne authority, without any further staying (as they had done) for the ciuill Magistrate, albeit they pretende now the contrary: then it is fit that I produce some further matter to this purpose.

Amongst sundry things in the said booke of *Discipline*, let these few be well considered-of, & weighed. It is there sayd: *Presbyterium in singulis ecclesiis constituendum est, there ought to be erected in euery Church a Presbyterie.* Now if they had meant, (as it is pretended) not to haue put their book, or at the least some chiefe parts thereof in practise, vntill it should haue beene established by *Act* of *Parliament*, they would haue sayde for *constituendum est*, there ought to bee erected, *constituatur*, let there bee erected in euery parish a Presbyterie.

Againe, in all their assemblies prescribed in the booke, this was one point to be still inquired-of: *vtrum disciplina vigeat, whether the Discipline had any life in it, or were esteemed, or continued:* which question had beene friuolous, and very vnmeete to haue beene continued, as prescribed by Law, if the Discipline it selfe had beene allowed by *Act* of *Parliament*, before that question should haue beene moued. Cap. de conuent. ecclesiæ.

Furthermore saith the booke: *in funeribus desuescendum est commodè, ab habendis concionibus, quod periculum sit, ne superstitionem quorundam foueant, aut vanitati inseruiant: The Preachers must leaue-of by little and little, as they may conueniently, to preach at burials, least thereby they nourish the superstition of some men, or giue ouer themselues to the preseruation of vanity.* Cap. de concionibus ad ecclesiam habendis.

Likewise, *festi dies sunt commodè abolendi: holy daies* (as we tearme them) *must be abolished*, commodè, *as they may, handsomely*. Nowe, if this booke had not beene meant, to

haue

haue beene put in practise in these two pointes, before it had come forth, authorised by law: they would haue said for the reasons alledged: *from henceforth let there be, or it is ordered, that there shall be no more preaching at burials, nor holy dayes obserued, or let them henceforth be abolished.*

Cap. de reliqui. Liturg. officiis.

Moreouer: *reliquæ liturgiæ tota ratio in sacramentorum administratione, & ex vsu ecclesiæ in nuptiarum benedictione consistit. Cuius forma commodissima est, quæ ab ecclesiis vsurpatur, quæ disciplinam ex Dei verbo instaurârunt. The rest of the* liturgy *doth consist in the administration of the Sacraments, and (as the vse of the Church is,) in blessing of marriages. The forme whereof, is most fit and commodious, that is vsed by those Churches, which haue erected the* discipline, *according to the worde of God.*

In the *Parliament* (27. of her Maiestie: as I remember) the brethren hauing made another booke, tearmed at that time: *A booke of the forme of common prayers, &c.* and contayning in it the effect of their whole pretended discipline: the same booke was penned, altogether statute and law-like, and their petition in the behalfe of it was: vz. *May it therefore please your maiesty, &c. that it may be enacted, &c. that the booke hereunto annexed, &c. intituled: a booke of the forme of common prayers, administration of Sacraments, &c. and euery thing therein contained, may be from henceforth authorized, put in vre, & practised throughout all your maiesties dominions.* See here, when they hoped to haue attained their purposes by law, and to haue had the same accordingly established: they offered to the *Parliament* a booke of their own, for the *forme* of *common praiers, &c.* and thought it (as it seemeth) altogether inconuenient, to leaue euery minister to his owne choyse, to vse what forme hee list, other then such as were allowed in some Church, which had receiued the Discipline: for any such they liked-of indefinitly.

Whereby

Whereby it to me it seemeth manifest, that they neuer meant, to haue required the enacting of that Chapter, *de reliquis liturgiæ officijs*, but onely to set downe, what course their bretheren should follow for the *interim*, vntill they might take further order for a booke of their owne.

Lastly, in all this whole booke of *Discipline*, there is not once mention made of any authority, or office, in or ouer the Church; belonging to the Christian *ciuill* Magistrate. Hee hath not so much, as either voyce or place, in any of their *Synodes*, as a member thereof: except he be chosen to be an *Elder*. He hath not any power assigned vnto him to call a *Synode*: no, though it bee a *Nationall Synode*: nor so much as to appoint the particular times or places of their meetinges, nor (which is most strange,) so much as that his assent, is to be required to any of their Canons. But all these thinges are set downe in this booke, as of right to appertaine vnto their Ministers and Elders. For the tryall whereof: I must needes referre you to the booke it selfe, which is in many mens handes: where you shall finde the brethren ascribe that to themselues, which in the greatest darkenes of Popery, all the BB[s]. in the Land (for ought I doo remember) durst neuer challenge. Which is a proofe sufficient, that either they meant by cunning to haue depriued her Maiesty, by her owne consent, of all her *regall* authority, in these and such like causes of the Church, as not of right belonging vnto her (which they will not acknowledge:) or otherwise, that they had agreed without her consent, to take this authority vnto themselues: which (if they had any conscience) they would not stick to confesse: that being assuredly their currant doctrine, as in some other place it shall hereafter more fully appeare.

But it may be said that these are onely collections. Well let them be, as they are. Indeede there is no cause, why I ſhould ſtand vpon collections, hauing yet in ſtore moſt euident demonſtrations.

Chap. XI.

Further proofe for their practiſe of their Diſcipline out of the articles they ſubſcribed.

Here hath beene often mention made, of the articles, whereunto the brethren ſubſcribed, for their allowance and practiſe of the ſayd booke of *Diſcipline:* and they are worde for worde, as here I doo ſet them downe, according to the depoſition of thoſe, that ſubſcribed vnto them, and as they are to bee ſhewed vnder Maiſter *Wights* hand.

We the brethren aſſembled together, in the name of God, hauing heard and examined, by the word of God, according to our beſt abilitie and iudgement in it, a draught of diſcipline eſſential, *and neceſſary for all times, and Synodicall, gathered out of the Synodes, and vſe of the Churches; haue thought good to teſtifie, concerning it, as followeth.*

We acknowledge and confeſſe the ſame, agreeable to Gods moſt holy word, ſo farre as we are able to iudge or diſcerne of it, excepting ſome fewe pointes, which wee haue ſent to our Reuerend brethren of this aſſembly, *for their further reſolution.*

We affirme it to be the ſame, which wee deſire to be eſtabliſhed in this Church, by daily praier to God: which we promiſe (as God ſhall offer oportunity, and giue vs to diſcerne it ſo expedient) by humble ſuit vnto her Maieſties honourable Councell, and the Parliament, and by all other lawfull and conuenient meanes, to further and aduance, ſo farre as the lawes, and peace, and the preſent eſtate of our Church, will ſuffer it, and not enforce to the contrary.

We

We promise to guide our selues, and to be guided by it, and according to it.

For more especiall declaration of some points more important and necessarie, we promise uniformely, to follow such order, when we preach the word of God, as in the booke by vs is set downe, in the Chapters *of the office of Ministers of the word, of preaching or sermons, of Sacraments, of Baptisme, and of the Lords supper.*

Further also, wee promise to followe the order set downe in the Chapters *of the meetings, as farre as it concerneth the Ministers of the worde. For which purpose, we promise to meete euery sixe weekes together, in* Classicall *conferences, with such of the brethren here assembled, as for their neighbourhood may fit vs best: and such other, as by their aduise we shall be desired to ioyne with vs.*

The like wee promise, for Prouinciall *meetinges euery halfe yeare from our conferences, to sende vnto them, as is set downe in the* Chapter, *concerning the* Prouinces, *and the conferences belonging vnto them, beeing deuided according to the order following.*

Likewise also, that we will attend the generall assembly *euerie yeare, and at all* Parliaments, *and as often as by order it shall be thought good, to be assembled.* Hitherto the Articles.

Now by these articles, and by their subscription vnto them, it is most euident, that the pretences made by some, are but meerly shiftes: as that their purpose onely was, to haue the booke in readines against a *Parliament*, and that they subscribed the articles to no other ende, but onely to testifie their agreement in iudgement, for that they were charged to disagree amongst themselues. For if that had beene their intent, it had beene sufficiently performed, by subscribing to the first article onely. But they proceede-on further: and entred into a certaine *league*, or *association*, binding themselues by promise; vnder their hands, what they (for their owne partes) will attempt, and as they might perfourme.

In the second article, (as it is apparant,) there are other lawfull meanes promised to bee vndertaken, (for the aduancing of the *Discipline*,) then *prayers* to God, and *supplications* to her Maiesty and the Parliament. Whereupon *Maister Litleton* (a subscriber) being examined, what hee vnderstoode *those meanes to bee*: answereth vpon his oath, *that he thinketh their priuate conferences, were meant, to be those lawfull meanes mentioned in the article*. Which is according to the resolution of the brethren in of *London*, set downe before, out of *Maister Edmondes* examination: vz. *that seeing they could not preuaile, by sute to the State: the Ministers themselues should set vp the* Discipline, *as they should bee able*. And *Maister Iohnson*, is also as direct vppon his oath, to the same effect, saying.

Litleton.

Before the Commissioners.

Before the Commissioners.

It was a generall conclusion amongst all the Classes, *and brethren, that forasmuch, as the* Discipline *required by petitions, could not bee publikely established by lawe, it was thought in conscience necessary, to establish it and practise it priuately: to which purpose also, euery man was to vse his endeuour, to encrease the number of such, as would conforme themselues that way.*

Againe it is promised in the same *Article*, that they would proceede with their sayd meanes, for the aduancement of their *Discipline*, *so far as the peace of the present state of our Church would suffer.*

Now how farre that is, it hath beene before touched in the *decrees* of one of their *Synodes*, *1583*. for as men most strangely bewitched) they imagined, that they could so cunningly play their feates, as that they (might in effect) set vp their owne *Discipline*, secretely, vnder hand, and yet neuer disturbe the present gouernement of the Church.

For as peace is heere taken in their sense, one King or

gouerne-

gouernement may inuade another, with all kinde of hostility, and say (as they doo) that they meane but peace. The truth is, they may haue peace in their mouths, but in their actions, there is nothing lesse. So as this their restraint (being but a vaine pretence) doth no way indeed impeach my assertion.

Furthermore, whereas also it followeth in the same article, *(and not enforce to the contrarie,)* Maister *Littleton* being examined vpon his oath *what that should meane:* answereth that he *himselfe, Maister Snape, Maister Proudloe, and others did agree, to put the said articles and* Discipline *in execution and practise, so far as the peace and the present estate of the Church will suffer, and not enforce to the contrarie. That is to say: till the Magistrate did enioyne them or enforce them, to leaue the practise of the said* Discipline: and in another place, *till the Magistrate did inhibite them to the contrarie, and force them to leaue it.* And further, hee also sayth: *that they did agree to guide themselues by the said booke of Discipline, and according to it, with the same limitation.* Now what if by their secret practises, (to drawe away the peoples harts from the present gouernement of the Church) they could haue procured such strength and number, to haue followed them, as that no reasonable restraint, or force of the Magistrate had bin able to haue encountred and suppressed them? I doo but aske the question.

In the Starre Chamber.

In the rest of the *Articles*, there are but two generall points: the one contained in the third *Article*, concerning the vniformitie, which they promise to vse in their Ministery: and the other is, as touching their agreement, to follow the orders set downe for their meetinges: *Classicall*, contained in the fourth: *Prouinciall* in the fift: *Nationall* in the sixt article.

So as where before in the second *Article*, they had mentioned *other meanes*, whereby they had promised to aduance their *Discipline*, besides *praiers to God*, and *supplications to her Maiestie*: they doo nowe in part explane themselues, in the other *Article* following, and doo set downe, what *meanes* they that were Ministers would vse and put in practise, for the aduauncement of it, vz. the two points mentioned, that is, their *vniformity in preachings*, and their *meetinges*: according to Maister *Littletons* deposition: in these words: *they meant by those meanes, in the second Article, their conferences, as he thinketh*. But to carry this matter past thinking: let Master *Fen* be heard: who saith: *that he agreed to put some things of the booke in execution, according to the subscription*: let Master *Lord* be heard: who sayth, *that he agreed to put some things of the said booke in practise, as in the Articles is contained*. But let their *Coryphaeus* Maister *Cartwright* himselfe be heard: who sayth, *that he agreed to put two points of the Articles in execution*: *vz. touching the order of preaching, and touching the assemblies.*

In the Starre Chamber.

Chap. XII.

It is confessed that they agreed to put one point of their booke in practise without her Maiesties assent: what it is: & of strange names giuen to children.

NOw because it appeareth, in the thirde, fourth, fift and sixt of the sayd *Articles*, that concerning both these points, they referre themselues to certain *Chapters* of their booke of *Discipline*: I haue thought it very conuenient, to set downe, out of the said *Chapters*, some of those particulars, which by their said subscription they bound themselues to practise, without any further staying for the ciuil Magistrate: and withall to adioyne some part of their constancie, (if so I may abuse

abuse a good worde,) in the perfourming of their promises, touching the said particulars, Maister *Littleton* beeing sworne, dealeth (as it seemeth) very directly to this purpose: for (as he saith) concerning the contents of the foure last *Articles, hee for his part, whilest hee was of that company, perfourmed his promise, and (he thinketh) that the rest that subscribed did the like.* But to the particulars: and first of the first point.

Exami. befor the Commi

The Minister, that is to preach, shall appoint the Psalme that is to be song, &c. After the Psalme, let there be made a short admonition to the congregation: howe they shall prepare themselues rightly, to pray. Let a Prayer followe, containing the confession of sinnes, &c. and concluded with the Lords Prayer. After the Sermon, let Prayers be made for grace, that the auditors may profite by the doctrine deliuered: also for the whole Church, and all particular callinges: and let them end likewise with the Lords Prayer. Then a Psalme, &c. and lastly let the conclusion bee made, with some short forme of blessing the congregation, taken out of the Scriptures.

De officio. Minist. &c

For the practise of this order: I referre the proofe of it to all those, who haue obserued the manner of any of the brethrens behauiour, in their seuerall Churches. The most of them, that are but Doctors, (as they terme themselues) and readers of Lectures in other mens charges, do seldom or neuer come to the seruice, which is read in the Church according to her Maiesties Lawes: but vnder pretence of studying for their sermons, doo absent themselues, vntill seruice bee done, or at the least almost finished, and then they come in, (grauely I warrant you,) and doo goe to this their owne forme of seruice.

The rest of the fraternity, that haue cures of their own, some of them will haue a *Parliament Minister*, (as they terme him) vnder them, to say seruice: and then he himselfe

selfe dealeth, as it hath beene noted of the Doctor: but others, that are not able to haue such a one, they for their *safer standing* (as their tearme is) doo vse some piece of our seruice-booke, and peraduenture reade a lesson, (which things they affirme, as it hath beene touched, may be performed as wel by those, that are not ministers, as by them.) And then they in like sort, doo begin their owne ministeriall function, and proceede according to the foresaide fashion, subscribed vnto, and promised.

But to proceede vnto their practise of other pointes of that booke.

De concionibus habendis, &c.

The Preachers must leaue off, by little and little, as they may conueniently, to preach at burials, least thereby they nourish the superstition of some men, or giue ouer themselues to the preseruation of vanity.

De Baptismo.

Let not women onely offer infants to Baptisme, but the father, if it may be conueniently, or els some others in his name.

Let perswasions be vsed, that such names, as doo sauour either of Paganisme or Popery, bee not giuen to children at their Baptisme, but principally those, whereof there are examples in the Scriptures.

Whether these pointes, (especially for two of them) haue beene practised by the brethren or not, the *newe Churchyard* in *London*, and many brables in the country, about vrging of the natural fathers to become Godfathers to their owne children, &c, can more then sufficiently witnesse. And for the third, it is also sundry waies apparant. For whence else doo these new names and fancies proceede? *The Lord is nere. More-tryall. Reformation. Discipline. Ioy-againe. Sufficient. From-aboue. Free-gifts. More-fruite. Dust.* and many other such like. But *Richard Hawgar* of *Northampton*, did first vnder his hande, and after vpon his oath, deliuer an especiall history (to this purpose) of

Fenner. Barbon. Aire. Wigginton. &c. Before the Commissioners.

of giuing names.

Snape *would not Baptise one* Christopher Hodgkinsons *childe, because hee would haue the childe called* Richard. *The order was this.* Hodgkinson *obtained promise of* Snape: *that he would christen his childe. But (saith* Snape*) you must then giue it a Christian name, allowed in the Scriptures. The partie told him, that his wiues father, whose name was* Richard, *desired the name. Well (saith* Snape*) you must doe as I bidde you: that, when you come, the congregation be not troubled. But notwithstanding, the said* Hodgkinson *not thinking it would haue beene made a matter of such importance, the child was brought.* Snape *proceeded in the action, till hee came to the naming of the child. And when he heard, that they called the child* Richard, *& that they would giue him no other name; hee staied there, and would not in any wise Baptize the child. And so the child was carried away thence, & was Baptized the weeke following, at* Alhallowes *being named* Richard.

Of likelyhoode, the brethren haue founde this thing to be a matter of great importance: that they wil rather leaue an infant vnbaptized, then giue him such a name.

Chap. XIII.

A second point of their Booke confessed to be agreed vpon, for the practise of it, without her Maiesties assent.

Now I wil come to Master *Cartwrights* second point, that is, of the *meetings*: and set downe the Chapters, whereunto in the *Articles* subscribed, they referred themselues: that thereby herafter no man, that wil read them, may doubt of their purpose, of not staying for the Magistrate: which are as follow, so neere as

I could by translation of them out of Latin, expresse their meaning.

Of the assemblie of the Church.

Mutuall conference is to bee practised in the Church by common assemblies: but in these, matters Ecclesiasticall are to bee handled, and such chieflie as concerne those Churches, whereof the assemblie doth consist.

They shall not determine, (except they be requested,) of anie thing touching other Churches: but shall only decree, that such matter is to be referred to the next greater assemblie: Let the matters and order of thinges to be handled in them be thus.

Next after the view or calling of those that be present, (wherin withall, the names of such as bee absent must be noted, that in the next Assembly, they may eyther yeeld sufficient reason of their absence, or els bee censured, by the iudgement of the assemblie,) first let the Acts of the next assemblie afore, (that was of the same sort) bee read: to the intent, that if any thing of them were left then vndone, it may be dispatched. Then, let those matters be done, that are peculiar to the Assembly in hand. And first, let euerie of them deliuer the instructions from their Churches, in the same order that they sit, together with the Fiduciary *or Letters of credence of the Churches: next, let there be** censures *had of the Churches of that assembly: whereby may bee vnderstood how they are framed and vsed: whether the doctrine and the Discipline haue their course in them, and whether the officers of them doe that which appertaineth, and such like.*

*vz. inquisition (as I take it) is meant.

Besides let them decree those things, that shall concerne eyther the common behoofe of all the Churches of that assemblie, or of any one of them: and this course will be sufficient enough, for the view and ouersight of the Churches.

Lastly, (if it so seeme good) let there bee inquirie & Censures had, euen of those, which be delegated to meete in that Assemblie.

Such as are to meete in the Assemblies, let them bee chosen, by the Suffrages of those Churches or Assemblies, that haue interest

or

or to doe in it: and out of these, let such only be chosen, as hath exercised some publike office in that Church, eyther of a Minister, or of an Elder, and which hath subscribed both to the doctrine and Discipline, and which haue vndertaken to behaue themselues in all things according to the word of God.

It shall be lawful for other Elders & Ministers, yea & for Deacons and Students in Diuinitie, by the appointment of the assemblie, (especially if they be such, as doe exercise themselues, in interpreting the Scriptures in the Assemblie,) to be both present, & to bee asked their iudgements: these of the latter sort are therefore to be admitted, that their iudgements to handle the affaires of the Church, may hereby both be tried and sharpned. Yet let none be counted to haue a voice, but those onely, that were chosen by the Church, & which bring their commissions consigned vnto them.

If any matter be to bee consulted of, that is of speciall importance, let the President of the last superior Assembly, or the Minister of that Church, in which the next Assembly is to be made, send it ouer in due time vnto the Ministers of all the churches of that assemblie: to the intent they may afore treate thereof, with those of their charge, and so may know and report their iudgements. In making choise of a place for the Assemblies, respect is to be had of neerenes, and other oportunities: in case any party may iustly finde himselfe grieued aboue the rest.

It is expedient, that in euerie Ecclesiasticall Assembly, there be a President, which may gouerne the assembly, and that he bee from time to time chaunged, if it may be conueniently: & he must be thus chosen, viz.

He that was President of the last Assemblie of that kinde afore, or the Minister of that congregation, where the Assemblie is made, (conceiuing first a praier directed to that purpose) shall preferre vnto the Assemblie, the motion for choise of a President.

The President *beeing thus chosen, conceiuing first a Prayer fitting vnto the whole action and Assembly,) shall call ouer the names of those, which be present and which bee absent, and note them: that the absents may be called-vpon at the next assembly, to yeeld a reason of their absence.*

Which if it be not sufficient, let them be censured, by the authoritie of the Assemblie. Then let him read the Actes of the last Assembly, that if any thing thereof remaine, it may then bee dispatched. Then shall he aske of euerie one in order as they sit, their letters fiduciarie *or of credence, and their instructions signed. Which being propounded in the same order, and sufficiently debated by all their opinions, hee shall aske their iudgements, and gather the suffrages, and pronounce what the greater part adiudgeth. Which he shall procure to be put into Actes, that the Delegates of the seuerall Churches, may procure copies and transcripts to bee made, which they may impart vnto those Churches, to whome it appertaineth.*

The President *also, by the iudgement and authority of the Assembly, is to giue answere, either by word of mouth, or by letters, to such as require it. If any censures be to be inflicted, hee is to performe them. He shall also take care, that all things be godly and quietly carried, by exhorting them vnto quietnes, and moderation of minde, one bearing with another, as neede shall bee, and by preferring vp, such as be wilfull and contentious, vnto the Assembly: lastly, he shall propound vnto them, touching the time of their next meeting: and then with exhortation vnto them, chearefully to goe forward in their ducty, and with thanksgiuing, he shall curteously dismisse them.*

Before the dismission of the Assembly, let no man depart, but with leaue.

The assemblies according to their seuerall kindes, if they bee greater, are of more; if they be lesse, they are of lesse authoritie. Therefore it is lawfull to appeale from a lesse assemblie to a greater,

ter, if any man thinke he haue iniurie, except the fact be most euident and plaine vnto euery man: but yet none otherwise, but that the iudgement of the assemblie shall hold, vntill it shall be otherwise adiudged, in an assemblie of greater authoritie.

Assemblies are eyther { Classes, *or* Synods.

Classes *are conferences of the fewest Ministers of Churches, standing neare together, as for example of twelue.*

The chosen men of all the seuerall Churches of that assembly, are to meete in conference; that is to say, for euery Church a minister and an Elder: and they shall meete euerie fortnight. They shall chiefly endeuour the ouersight and censure of that Classis*: searching particularly, whether in them euery thing be done, according to the holy doctrine and discipline of the Gospell: vz. Whether any question bee arisen, touching any point of doctrine.*

Whether the Ecclesiasticall discipline haue his course.

Whether any Minister be wanting in any of the Churches, that they may speedily prouide a fit person.

Whether the rest of the Elders and Officers of the Church, bee appointed in euery Church.

Whether care be had, ouer schollers, and the poore.

In what pointes the Classes *doo want aduise, for the further aduancing of the Gospell among them.*

Before they make an ende, let some of the Ministers present, make a sermon, either in course, or being chosen thereto by voyces. Of whome the rest of the Ministers (secluding the Elders) shall iudge among themselues: and if in any point, it shall be requisite, they shall monish him brotherly: weighing euery thing, according to the course, afore laid-downe in the Chapter, touching those things, which are to be performed by him that preacheth to the congregation.

Synodes.

A Synode *is an assembly of chosen men, from moe Churches, then those that be in one* Classis, *or conference.*

In these, the Articles of the holy Discipline and Synodicall, must alwaies be read: also in them, (after all other thinges be finished,) censures or inquisition made, vpon all that be present: and the supper of the Lorde shall bee celebrated by them, in and with that congregation, where the Assembly is made, if conueniently it may be.

Of Synodes there be two sortes: the first is particular, and this conteineth vnder it both Prouinciall *and* Nationall Synodes.

A Prouinciall Synode, *is an assembly of those, which bee delegated from all the* Classes *or conferences of that Prouince.*

Let euery Prouince conteine in it 24. Classes.

This may be a fitte order, for the assembling together of a Synode Prouinciall. *vz. Let this care be laid vpon some certaine Church, by consent of the Synode: let that Church, with aduise of the* Classis *whereof it is, prefixe the place and time for the Assembly: let other Churches, sende vnto such Church, those matters which seeme vnto them of some difficultie to determine: and likewise those matters, that doo appertaine to the whole* Prouince, *and that diligently in conuenient season: to th'intent, that that Church may in due time giue aduertisement vnto all the* Classes *of the Prouince, both of the time and place, and of the matters to be handled: so that such as are sent, may come better prepared, & and that they may iudge thereof, according to the resolution of their*

their owne seuerall Classes or conferences.

Let euery Classis sende vnto the Prouinciall Synode two Ministers, and as many Elders.

It shall bee called euery halfe yeare, or more often, vntill the Discipline be confirmed.

But before a Nationall Synode be celebrated, let it be called three months afore, that they may prepare, and furnish vp those things, that belong vnto it.

Let the Acts of all the Prouinciall Synodes be sent vnto the Nationall, by that Church, in which the Prouinciall assembly was had: and let euery Minister be furnished, with the copies of the Acts, and with the reasons vsed.

The Nationall, is a Synode consisting of the Delegats from all the Synods Prouincail, that are within the dominion of one common-wealth. Let the manner of calling it, be the same, that is appointed for calling the Prouinciall, except the Synode it selfe shall take other order herein: vz: by some certaine Church: yet so, as the said Church doe appoint for place and time (to holde it in) such as the Prouinciall Synode of that Church, which shall next ensue, shall determine, and thinke good.

For the Nationall Synode, three Ministers and three Elders must be chosen, out of euery Synode Prouinciall.

In it, the common affaires of all the Churches of the whole nation and kingdome, are to be handled: as of Doctrine, Discipline, and ceremonies: causes not decided in inferiour Assemblies, Appellations, and such like.

By the decree of the Nationall Synode, one is to be chosen, which shall reduce the commentaries or Actes of all the seuerall Churches, into one body.

Hitherto concerning particular assemblies. Now followes the vniuersall or œcumenicall Synode of the whole world.

And

And this is the Synode, that consisteth and is gathered together, of the chosen men out of euery particular Nationall Synode.

The Acts of all Synodes, are to be reduced into one body.

And thus farre these Chapters of the *meetings:* the particular points whereof, maister *Cartwright*, and his companions, haue bound themselues, by their subscriptions, to put in practise, without any further expectation for her Maiesties assent. And according to these pointes, (as their numbers and oportunities haue serued their turnes) they haue accomplished their bonds and promises; as by that which hath beene saide, and by depositions vppon othes, concerning their meetinges and dealinges in them, is most apparant, to any that is not blinded with wilfull obstinacie.

Chap. XIIII.

Moe points of their booke put in practise: fasts: calling of Ministers: presbyteries: censures, &c.

Vrthermore also, they haue not contented themselues with the execution of these thinges onely, but they haue besides proceeded, in like manner, with the ful practising almost of all the rest of the booke.

It is most notorious, that according to the doctrine thereof, they haue taken vppon them, to appoint publicke fasts: and then especially they haue done it, when their fellowes haue beene most busie, to trouble the present estate of the Church. Besides that, these fasts with their seueral sermons and other prophecyings,

ings, haue had another principal vse: vz. (as *Lord* did write to *Fen* of maister *Cartwrights* pleasure) *that the day following, the brethren might talke of other matters.*

Likewise (saith maister *Iohnson*) touching the election and making of ministers, *I thinke they obserue, asmuch as they can, the order prescribed in the said booke of Discipline. As about* Proudloe, *of* Weedenbeck *his admission, (as I haue heard) and* Snapes *and* Larkes. *The manner whereof is, that they renounce the calling, they haue had of the Bishops, and doe take it againe, from the approbation of the* Classis. And againe: *they will be content to accept orders from the Bishop, as a ciuill matter, but doe not thereby account themselues Ministers, vntill the godly brethren of some* Classes *haue allowed them.* But more fully *Richard Hawgar. The first degree they haue entered into, is this: that teaching all Ministers, which are called according to the order of the Church of England, to bee vnlawfull: they doe vrge, such as they dare trust, and who are Ministers alreadie) to seeke at their* Classis *a new approbation, which they terme the* Lords ordinance.

Iohnson before the Cōmissioners.

Rich. Hawgar his depositiō.

In this action, the Minister before allowed of, must renounce his former calling, and take that calling, (wherby he must stand) of them.

The manner whereof, is this: when any doe yeeld hereunto, they appoint a day of their Classis, *&c: As the example following wil shew. One master* Hocknel, *being to haue a benefice, was willed (by his Patrone) to bring some testimoniall, of the Ministers of the shyre for his good conuersation. Wherevpon hee came to Maister Snape. Who dealt with him (as is afore mentioned,) and* Hocknell *hauing beene a Minister before, (some sixe or seauen yeares) yeelding:* Snape, *with his companions gaue him a text, and appointed him a day.*

At which time the Classis met in Saint Peters: and hee preached. After, they assembled themselues, willing Hocknell to stand aloofe. Then Maister Penry beganne to make a speech, exhorting them to be carefull, to call vpon God: to deale without affectiō in this their action, &c. After which, they fel to the matter. Some liked, that the man shuld be admitted, & some otherwise. Those that were against him made these two reasons. First, that hee had not iumped meete, in deliuering the Metaphore, which was in his text: secondly because he was neyther Grecian nor Hebrician. So as they ouerruling the rest, Hocknell was called for, and in some sort commended: but yet the speaker of the Classis told him, he must take more paines at his book, before they could allow of him, as a fit Minister. Hereupon Master Hocknell and they fell out: and he (contemning their censure) did proceede, and tooke possession of his benefice.

When they call a man, that is not alreadie a Minister: then hauing vsed the order before mentioned, they command him to goe to the Bishops, as to a ciuile Magistrate, for his writinges, (which they tearme by a prettie name that this ex. hath forgotten: and this they say, is onely for his safe standing in his former calling, receiued of them: not that thereby hee receaueth any power to be a Minister. On this sort was Master Lark (dwelling a little from Wellingborow) called.

After this calling by them, the parties so called, may preache here and there, as he thinketh good, vntill hee bee called to a charge: & then he must go to the Bishop, for his better standing, and so the people calling him, he is a full Minister.

Maister Snape being a Minister already, renounced that his first calling: was called by the Classis: by that calling hee preached, but would not administer the Lords Supper. After the parish of Saint Peters knowing, that he must not account himselfe *a full Minister, vntill some particular congregation, had chosen him, they chose him for their Minister, and so he standeth at this present.* Thus farre *Hawger.*

It is likewise deposed by two, that Maister *Snape* for the answering of a question propounded vnto him, said, that *rather then he would haue stood, by vertue of any Letters of orders, he would haue bin hanged vpon the gallowes.* Rich. Holmes. Rich. Hawgar before the Cõmissioners.

But let Maister *Snape* speake himselfe. *Touching the substance of my calling to the ministerie: I affirme, that I had it of the church of God, being approued by the learned & godly neighbour Ministers, and chosen by the people of my charge, to that function. Touching that allowance, that I had of the Bishop, I take it to be a thing meerely ciuile, belonging to a ciuile Magistrate: which authoritie he hath by Act of Parliament, & which therefore I might lawfully receaue at his hands, for the peaceable execution of my Ministery.* Snape is a writing of his owne hand.

Againe, concerning the *Presbyteries*, (which the booke affirmeth shuld be in euery parish:) they (want in effect) nothing of all their whole platforme: if they could but once attaine vnto the publike erecting vp of those *thrones.* And how far it is likely they haue already preuailed therin, without staying any longer for her Maiestie; let these thinges following, whereof some haue beene touched alreadie, make it knowne vnto you. Mention hath beene made of a *Presbytery* set vp at *Wandesworth.* It was a decree of the London brethren, *that the Ministers should by little & little, as much as possibly they might, draw the Discipline into practise, though they concealed the names, eyther of Presbytery, Elder or Deacõ, making little account of the names for the time, so their offices might secretly be established.* There was an order sette downe, in an assembly (1583. as I take it) *for the conuerting of Churchwardens and Collectors, into Elders* Ma. Edmonds

ders and Deacons: as before in the Actes themselues it appeareth. According to this order the brethren afterward sent their directions abroad, to their fellowes, for their execution of it. *I receiued* (saith Master *Barbon*) *from our faithfull brother Maister* Gelibrande, *a direction of the brethren, concerning the Conuerting of Churchwardens into Elders, and Collectors into Deacons.* Richard Holmes affirmeth that *by such speeches as he hath heard, hee doth verily thinke, that the Ministers in their* Classes *haue resolued, to erect vp their seuerall Presbyteryes, in their owne parishes.* With him agreeth Master *Iohnson: according to the rules of that booke, I thinke that sercetly in most places, where the brethren of the* Classes *are, there are Elders chosen, and that they put the Discipline in practise, so farre as they may, amongst themselues, without any apparant shew thereof, to the ouerthrow of their* safe-standing. Further also he deposeth, that *he himselfe hath beene blamed diuers times, priuatelie, in that he would make no such choise of Elders, (where he preached,) to practise the Discipline.* And what els should *Gellibrand* meane, by these words in a Letter to *Field? I haue written to Maister Cartwright seuerally, and ioyntly to him and the Elders, signifying my readines, and what aduersaries there are.*

Barbon to Field.

Holmes.

Iohnson.

Lastly there was a nomination of Elders, at *Kilsby* in *Northampton-shiere*, made by Maister *Lee* the Pastor, in the yeare 1588. Their names as it was deposed before Sir *George Farmer* and Sir *Iohn Spencer*, were, *William Greene, Roger Cowley, Thomas Hall, Richard Wolfe, Iohn Browne,* and *William Mariat: which sixe (saith the deponent,) Maister* Lee *thought sufficient to determine and end all matters of controuersie in the said towne.* Henry Pinson *also affirmeth, that he being enformed of this election of Elders (by the said* Browne, *and others) would not yeelde his consent thereunto, but said hee would stand to the lawes of this realme, appointed by her Maiestie.*

Ioh. Browne.

One

One especiall reason, (as it was enformed) why *Pinson* refused in this sort to ioyne with his neighbours, was: for that there should haue beene some punishment, inflicted by the said Elders vppon his sonne, for flinging a stone at *Elder-Mariats* window, which he would none of, but was faine to flie to her Maiesties lawes.

So here then it appeareth (in some sort,) whether the brethrẽ meant, to stay any more for the ciuile Magistrate, in erecting of their *Presbyteries*: then they confesse they did, concerning their *vniformitie* in Sermons and tripartite *meetings*.

Besides, it doth also appertaine to the further proofe of the said *Presbyteries*, that (as it seemeth) some of those censures haue beene vsed: for example, *excommunication:* Which (by the rules of the Discipline booke) are of right to be exercised by them. One *Bluet* a Minister (as I suppose) being excõmunicated (as it seemeth) did write a Letter to *Field* and *Egerton:* wherein hee is most earnest, that vpon his repentaunce hee might bee restored againe to the Church. *Woe is me* (saith he) *that I am cast out of your presence this day: but shame and sorrow is vnto the cause. And if this woe and shame did but touch the bodie, it were tollerable: for then at the day of death I should end my miserie, and no more heare the words of reproach. For now euery one that seeth mee, reprooueth me: and I am become a rebuke vnto all men. But this is not all. Woe is me, that there is a partition-wall, betweene heauen and my conscience, &c. If my offence may not bee passed by, without further confession: euen before God and his Church in* London, *will I lie downe and licke the dust at your feet, and confesse more against my selfe then any of you know.* Seuere *Catoes*, I warrant you. But is this the matter they contend for, for, that men may fall downe, and kisse their feete?

There is also another example to this effect, worthie of

your remembrance: one *La. Thomson* writeth in this sort of it. *I thinke of him as an vnsound member, vnfit to bee continued in the bodie, vnles he would be subiect to the gouernment of a bodie, especially the bodie of our sauing God.* The partie meant by *Thomson*, was (as I take it) maister *Wilcox*, the author of that *admonition*, which caused the first breaking-out, of all those troubles, that since haue ensued. This appeareth by foure letters, written about the yeare 1583. three of them from *Field* to *Wilcox*, and one from *Wilcox* to *Field*. What the cause was, though it bee expressed in one of the said Letters, I omit to rehearse it, no waies minding to touch any mans priuate behauiour or infirmities. But this I must tel you, that the brethren, (that is in *Thomsons* sense, *the body of our sauing God,*) were so displeased and angrie with him, that they suspended him from his Ministerie, and did vse their censure of *excommunication* against him.

If you aske mee how *Wilcox* tooke this course at their handes, I answere, euen as *Pinson* before named did, when his sonne should haue beene punished: hee disliked it so much, as that hee began to call their authoritie (for such kind of their proceedings,) in question, he refused to submit himselfe to their censures, and told *Field* plainely, *that he had bin dealt disorderly withall, both for matter and manner:* adding *that hee had perhaps concealed as great infirmities of* Fields, *and of some others, as his were.*

With these and many such like words *Field* was greatly prouoked, and for his owne part defied him. *Whereas* (saith hee) *for the hiding of your owne shame, you beginne to score vp my faults, which you say are sixe in number, as great as yours, if you should vtter them: I say it is no help to you, but testifieth that old pride, hipocrisie and malice, which long time hath lurked in that cankered heart of yours, &c. But I doe defie you, &c.*

&c. And for his refusing of their proceedinges: *you ought not* (saith *Field*) *so lightly to esteeme, that holy censure of the brethren, but in true repentance to haue hidden your face, &c.* Againe: *if God hath made you an instrument, to seeke for the aduancement of Christs Scepter: kisse it your selfe and bee subiect vnto it &c.* Againe, *if you loue Christ and his Church, before your owne glorie, and your owne sinnes haue shut vp your mouth: then be silent for euer.* And notwithstanding that *Wilcox* tooke exception to their authoritie, yet in the Letter wherein *Field* answereth that point, and many others, he beginneth thus. *The Lord Iesus open your eyes, and giue you such a true sence, and feeling of your sins, that howsoeuer you for) a time) be throwne to Sathan; in the end your soule may be saued, and you may feele assurance of eternall life, &c.*

What the issue of this matter was amongst them, I find it not. It seemeth that in the end, *Wilcoxe* for lacke of his former maintenance, (which was withheld from him by the brethrens procurement, & vpon perswasiön that after a time he should be restored to his ministerie againe, and in the meane space be relieued) he was faine to yeeld and to submit himselfe vnto their censure, (by them tearmed *the Scepter of Christ*.) Marrie still he thought himselfe to be hardly vsed, and after some time of expectation, desired (as it seemeth) to know, how long hee should vndergoe their heauie indignation. Whereunto *Field* answered thus. *The brethren thought meet to admonish you, vtterly to surcease. For how long or how short, mee thinkes you should not enquire, considering the circumstances: who know very well your selfe, that if an other were in your case, that no time can bee limited. Neuerthelesse, if you doubt the iudgement to bee too hard, that already is giuen, you may aske the priuate opinions of others your best friends, as of Master* Cartwright, *and M.* Thomson, *who are of mind that you are for euer disabled to that function, &c.*

CHAP. XV.

CHAP. XV.

They haue ioyned themselues into an association or brotherhood, and doe appropriate to their meetings the name of the Church.

a Barbon to Field. Pig to Field. Snape to Stone. b Barbon to Field. c D. Chapman to Field. d Pig to Field 1586. e Gellibrand from Oxford to Field. f Wake to Field. g Knewstub to Field. h Wade to Field. i Barbon to Field. k L. Thomson to Field. l Lord to Field. m Wigginton to Field. n D. Chapmã to Field. o Gellibrand to Field.

THere is often mention made, in the premises of the brethren, but yet in none other sense, thẽ they approriate to themselues, in sundrie of their writinges and Letters, as [a] *Salute the brethren. Salute the* [b] *reuerend brethren, Master Trauers, Chark Barber, Gardner, Egerton. Salute* [c] *our most reuerend brother Maister Cartwright. Salute* [d] *our reuerend brother Maister Cartwright, and the rest of the brethren. The* [e] *brethren salute you. Commend* [f] *me to all our brethren. Commend mee* [g] *to all the brethren with you: the brethren with vs here are in health. Commend* [h] *me to Maister Charke and Maister Trauers, with all the rest of the brethren. Remember* [i] *me to the brethren. Let him* [k] *be accounted among the brethren, as hee deserueth. I writ to my Mother, to speake to you and our good brethren, to prouide me of some honest brother, to Catechise my family. To* [l] *Maister Field, with the rest of the Godly Ministers, his brethren, in* London. *To his beloued* [m] *brother, Maister Field, and to all other his faithfull brethren, namely of the Ministery, at or about* London. *Our* [n] *brethren haue determined. I trust* [o] *you are so linked together, by the bond of brotherly loue, and the desire of the pure Discipline of the church, that nothing may sunder you. The brethren assembled: the Godly brethren: our pore brethren here, (at Oxford) do long to heare from you: and,* in the Articles whervnto they subscribed: *we the brethren, &c.*

Vppon the occasion of these termes, and many other such

such like: it is found out by examination, that this *Classicall* and reforming consort, with their followers; haue diuided themselues from all the rest of the ministerie, and *Christians* in *England*: and linked themselues into a newe brotherhood, with this lincke, vz. (as *Doctor Cricke* tearmeth it) *the desire of the pure Discipline*: thereby shewing themselues to be most notorious *Schismatickes*.

Cricke to Field.

When salutations are written, (saith *maister Iohnson*) *by the brethren that seeke reformation, as vnto the godly brethren: the meaning is, (as I euer tooke it) to such as haue submitted themselues vnto the holy Discipline*. Againe, *when the name brother, is giuen to ministers, it signifieth them to be of some* Classis, *for their consulting and setting vp of Christes kingdome: and when to the laitie, those that generally do ioyne with the ministers for the discipline, and doe euery of them submit themselues to a minister of some of the* Classis, *&c. And these, both ministers and people, are the godly brotherhood, denying the name properly of a godly brother or sister to any other*. The same also (in effect) hath he deposed in the *Starre-chamber*: where he further addeth, *that thus he thought himselfe, when hee was of that brotherhood, and that it was so commonly maintayned, both by him, and by the rest of the* Northampton Classis.

Iohnson.

And maister *Edmondes*, in like maner, hath deposed as much to the same purpose, both in the *Starre-chamber*, & before her Maiesties *Commissioners for causes ecclesiasticall*. *This* (saith he) *I do know, that when salutations were sent, or letters written to* London *from some Ministers abroad, as from* Fen *or* Cartwright, *&c. to maister* Field *& the rest, &c. therby was alwaies meant, properly, the ministers or the brotherhood of the Ministery in* London: *and when they vse the name or phrase of godly brethren, or sisters, or godly brotherhood or sisterhood, they meane generally both all the said Ministers, and likewise as many, as do depend vpon them for the cause of reformation. So*

Edmondes.

as the rest of the Ministers and people, who and wheresoeuer, that doe not ioyne with them, (as is before said) are altogether excluded out of their brotherhood: insomuch, as they will auoide the company of all other, as much as they can possibly, refusing eyther to buy or sell, or to eat or drinke with them.

Againe, it may not in any wise be omitted, that in their seuerall said letters & other writings, they vse oftentimes the name of the *Church*, and of the *Churches*: in as lewd a sence, as they do the name of brethren. Thus they write. *I know*[a] *the state of this Church: Make knowen to vs the state of the Church with you. Our Churches*[b] *are in danger of such, as hauing beene of vs, do renounce all fellowship with vs.*

a Snape to Field.
b Knewstub to Field.
c Knewstub to Field.

The[c] *hand of God is like to be heauy vpon our Churches here, if the malice of Sathan and his instruments be not preuented. A woman with vs, &c. sometimes thought to be a friend to Religion, &c: giueth it forth, that Maister* Walsh *had laid witchcraft vpon her. She would haue had him conuented, by some of the Iustices: but when he was once named she was repelled. Now she is come to* London *&c: She deuiseth newe matter against him, and against vs all, as that wee should haue had meetinges at her house &c. and that wee haue a priuate iurisdiction among our-selues, thinking that this will make her entrance vnto the* Archbishop, *or high* Commissioners *&c. I pray you first conferre with maister* Walsh: *and then deale, (as secretly as you may) to medicine these mischiefes.*

Good Iustice.

d Blake to Field.
e Gelibrand to Field.
f Rob. Bluet to Field and Egerton.
g Fenne to Field.

It is long[d] *since I heard from you,* (saith one Blake) *of the state of the Church of* London. Another, *By M.* West[e] *& M.* Browne, *you shall vnderstand the state of the Churches, wherein we are.* A third: *If my offence*[f] *may not be passed by, without a further confession, euen before God and his Church, in* London *will I lie downe, and licke the dust at your feete, and confesse &c.* A fourth: *I receiued a letter*[g] *from you in the name of the rest of the brethren: whereby I vnderstand your ioyning together, in*

choosing

choosing of my selfe, vnto the seruice of the Church, vnder the Earle *of* Leicester, &c. *I am ready to runne, if the Church command me, according to the holy decrees and orders of the discipline.* By these their speeches it appeareth, that as they haue cut off themselues from the fellowship of the rest of the *Christians* in *England*, by ioyning themselues into a seuerall brotherhood: so haue they already seduced her Maiesties subiects, by gathering them together into a new societie, whereunto they doe appropriat the name of the Church: as though all other Churches in the realme, were but as *Iewish Sinagogues* or heathenish assemblies. This is not, (you shall see) my bare collection: heare the witnesses, what they hereof haue deposed.

In these brethrens speaches of the Church or Churches: it is to be vnderstood, that by the Church *of* England, *they meane the Church according to humaine lawes and the Popes: which is ruled, (as they terme it) by an Antichristian gouernement. And by the* Godly Churches, *or the* Churches of God *in England, they meane such places, congregations, or assemblies, as doe embrace the reformation, and haue such a minister, as is of some* Classis. Iohnson.

Sometime also by the Church, (as the Church of God in London) *is meant the* Classis *of the brethren, or their Synods.* And so maister *Edmondes: when they vse these, or the like speaches,* Edmondes. *in their writing or otherwise: vz. the Church or Churches of God heere, wish this or that, or the Church in* London *hath done this or that: ther by they especially meane, the Ministers thēselues.*

But for the further clearing of this matter: because the chiefe *Rabbies* of this conspiracie, do themselues preach in our material Churches, it is to be obserued, that the parish where they preach, being assembled, is not the Church properly in their sence: but as many thereof onely, as are ioyned vnto them with that inuiolable bond mentioned:

vz: *the desire of the godly discipline:* and those furthermore, who leauing their owne *parish Churches*, doe come vnto them. As for example: The Church of God (forsooth) in the *Black Fryers*, doth consist, besides that parish, of a number of men and Marchauntes wiues, dispersed here and there throughout the whole Citie. Be content to hear the depositions, that are taken to like purpose. *Maister Snape affirmed* (as *Richard Holmes* and *Richard Hawgar haue deposed*): *that here one, & there one, picked out of the Prophane and common multitude, and put a-part to serue the Lord: maketh the Church of God, and not the generall multitude. Maister Iohnson* saith, *that the brethren of the laitie doe seldome come to their owne parish Churches, nor receiue the communion there, otherwise then they are compelled for feare of trouble. For they account those their pastors onely, whom they do so choose.* And maister *Edmonds*, vpon his experience in *London. The people of this brotherhood, do seldome come to their owne parish Churches, otherwise then for feare, to incurre some daunger of lawes: neyther do they accompt the minister of their parishes, to bee any of their pastors properly: except he be some one of the* brethren Ministers, *before specified, or very effectually inclining that way.*

Snape. Holmes. Hawgar.

Edmondes.

It is likewise to bee obserued, that if any of this faction, brotherhood, or sisterhood, do lie dangerously sicke: they do seldome or neuer, send for their owne pastors to visite them: nor moue them to pray for them, publikely. in their owne parish as neglecting their praiers: but do send to the Readers abroad, whom they haue chosen for their pastors, both to come vnto them, & to pray with them, and for them, in their assemblies.

This also is to bee obserued, that the stricter sort of this crue, when they lie at the point of death, will haue no bell tolled for them: and many of them do take order, before their death: that afterwardes, they be not buried in any Church: that there bee no sermon: nor any wanner of buriall vsed, which is prescribed.

Chap. XVI.

A ridiculous pretence of laws: with a recapitulation of the summe of this third booke.

S they countenance these their conuenticles, & vnlawful assemblies before specified, with the name of *the Church:* so with the like boldenesse, (to the same purpose) some of them are not ashamed to affirme: that by the doctrine of the Church of *England*, and by the lawes and statutes of this Realm, the present gouernment of the Church of *Englād*, vnder her Maiestie, by *Archbishops* and *Bishops*, is to bee accounted wicked and vnlawfull, and withall (in effect) that by the saide doctrine, lawes, and statutes, all the former proceedings, decrees, &c. of the brethren, are to be maintayned and iustified. As by the particular proofes following, it will appeare. Martin Iun.

The offices [a] *of Lord Archbishops and Bishops, &c.* (saith Martin Iunior) *are condemned, by the doctrine of the Church of England. The doctrine that condemneth the places of* Lorde Bishops *is* [b] *approoued by the statutes of this Realme, and her Maiesties prerogatiue royall. To be* [c] *a* Lord Bishop *is directly against the Statute:* 13. *Elizab. According* [d] *to the doctrine of the Church of England, our Prelates haue no authoritie to make Ministers, or to proceede to any ecclesiasticall censure: their* [e] *citations, processes, excommunications, &c. are neither to bee obeyed nor regarded. Men ought* [f] *not to appeare in their Courtes: a* [g] *man being excommunicated by them, ought not to seeke any absolution at their hands.* And in the behalfe of the brethren, he doth also further affirme: *that by the* [h] *said doctrine of the Church of England &c. all Ministers bee of equall authority*

a Martin Iun.
b *Thes.* 49
c *Thes.* 50
d Thes. 78.
e Thes. 82
f Thes. 83
g *Thes.* 84
h *Thes.* 72

iThes. 80. *authoritie: that the* [i] *godly ministers ought to ordaine those, that would enter into that function, without any leaue of the prelates, and not so much as once to suffer them to take any approbation of the prelates: that* [k] *euery minister is bound to preach the Gospell,*
k Thes. 85. *notwithstanding the inhibition of the* Bishops: *that* [l] *a man be-*
l Thes. 86. *ing once made a minister, is not to be kept backe from preaching,*
m Thes. 106. *by the inhibition of any creature: and* [m] *that by the saide doctrine, &c. all ministers are bound by subscription, &c. to disauow the* Hierarchie *of* Bishops.

When you shall reade these strange assertions, so farre passing any ordinary bounds of common modestie: think with your selues, that it is no maruaile, to see their writinges so full of authorities. For I do assure you, that euen in the like sort, and with the same sinceritie & faithfulnes, doe they alledge for their platformes, both Scriptures, Councels, Fathers and Histories.

Moreouer, what with the pretence of Gods law, of mans law, and (I know not) of what law, they haue been suffered to go so farre against all lawes: that now they haue taken such heart, as that some of them are not affraid to affirme (and that in print because the people might take notice of it): that there is no authoritie, which may lawfully suppresse their foresaid proceedinges. *No Magistrate (saith one*
Martin Iun. Thes. 17. 18. 22. *of the brotherhood) may lawfully mayme or deforme the body of Christ, which is the Church: no lawfull Church gouernment is changeable, at the pleasure of the Magistrate: of necessitie all christian Magistrates are bound, to receiue this gouernment, &c.*

And thus hitherto you haue seen the proceedings of our English reformers according to their ringleaders actions in Scotland: they haue had their draughts of discipline: they haue subscribed a particular book for England: they haue put their former platformes, & their said particular booke, (for the most part of it) in practise, as neare as they could:

they

they haue had their meetinges and *Synodes*, generally throughout all the lande: they haue made decrees & conclusions, not only to further their own conspiracy, but also to ouerthrow the present gouernment of the *Church*: they haue had in some places their *Elders*: they haue exempted themselues from the ecclesiasticall gouernment in this Realme, accounting the same, (in some respects,) to be *Antichristian*, and so not to be obeyed, (& in some other) to be a meere ciuile, and *a parliament church-gouernment*: and in that regard, onely after a sort, to bee yeelded vnto, for their better & *safer standing*, in their owne seditious and consistorian waies. They haue, by their false glosses, seduced many of her Maiesties subiectes: they haue combined themselues together, into a strange brotherhood. They challenge to their vnlawfull and seditious assemblies, the true and most proper name of *the Church*.

They say their doings are according to law.

They affirme (in effect) that no Magistrate may lawfully ouerthrow that, which they haue builded: inasmuch, as now it is saide, that the *Bishops, in seeking* by the authority which her Maiestie hath giuen and confirmed vnto them, to maintaine (as they are bound) the present church-gouernment and state, established by her highnes lawes within this Realme, and to suppresse and reforme their schismaticall & seditious disorders, and such like, are the disturbers of the peace of the church: that the Bishops beginne *the* [b] *quarrel* in disquieting of them, who *in towne and country, were very greatly at vnity, & tooke sweete councell together, for the profiting of the Church. That* [c] *the Bishops are the schismatickes, and not they: that the crime of schisme, which the prelates woulde fasten vppon them, doth iustly cleaue to the Bishops: and that* [d] *Bishops may be discharged by the Church.*

And they haue entred alreadie into this consideration, how

a The humble motion pa. 84.

b The humble motion pa. 84.

c Epistle to the discouerie of R B. &c.

d Register pa. 69

how Archbishops, Bishops, Chauncellors, Deanes, Cannons,
Lord to Fen. 1589. *Archdeacons, Commissaries, Registers, Apparitors &c. (All which, by their said pretended reformation, must be thrust from their liuings) should be prouided for, that the common wealth be not thereby pestred with beggars.*

Whereby it appeareth, that (in their owne conceites) they haue already attained their soueraintie. They and their conuenticles (forsooth) are the true Church: and all England besides is in a schisme.

So as now it may be dayly expected, when these godly brethren, for a full conclusion of their attempts, will take vpon them, (as their maisters did in *Scotland*) to discharge
Declaration B 2. the estate of *Bishops*, and to direct their commissioners, to her most excellent Maiestie, commanding both her and her highnesse most honourable *priuie Councell*, vnder the pain of excommunication, to appoint no *Bishops* hereafter, because they haue concluded that state to bee vnlawfull: and that furthermore her *Highnes*, vnder the same penaltie, shall not presume from thenceforth, either any longer to maintaine the present *Antichristian Church-gouernment*, or once to attempt the ouerthrowing of theirs. And thus much of this matter, vz. concerning our English reformers, and their imitation of the Ministers of *Scotland*, in that seeing they could not preuaile, with their suites & supplications to her Maiestie and the Parliament, for the setting vp of their discipline: they haue taken vpon them to doe it themselues.

The end of the third Booke.

THE FOVRTH BOOKE OF DISCIPLINARY GROVNDES and Practises.

CHAP. I.

Some of them seeme to growe desperate, and propound to themselues a strange example to follow, for the adauncing of their Discipline.

AS the Ministers of *Scotland* with their adherentes, finding sondry impedimentes in theyr foresaide proceedings, and in the setting-vp of their discipline, did grow to be very angry, & ther-vpon often-times before they came to armes or violence, did cast out many greate speaches and threatnings (as it hath beene before declared): euen so also it fareth now rightly, with our *Disciplinarians* in *England*. They threaten and bragge aboue measure, what shall come to passe: and I pray God they be suffered to go no further.

One of the brethren, (in the name of the rest,) complaining, that they are oppugned, and (as he saith) persecuted, desireth, *that the same may be prouided for*: and addeth ther-k.admonit. pa, 59. withall these words. *It is the case already of many a thousand in this land: yea it is the case of as many, as seeke the Lorde aright, &c. Greate troubles will come of it, if it be not prouided for.*

None seeke the Lord aright but this *brotherhood*. Great ioy of them. But what troubles meane they? That, an other seemeth to cleare: where he sayeth, that they can endure no such hard dealing, as is vsed against them any longer. *Alas* (saith hee) *wee are neuer able to stand against the pouerty, losses, imprisonment, discountenance, by our superiors, that our bretheren haue sustayned &c. Neuer able to swallow vp the slaunders, and bitter names of puritanes, precisians, traitors, seditious libellers &c.* Why? what will you doe?

Suppl. pa. 61,

The best that can bee gathered of his wordes, is this. *Come,* (saith hee) *let vs make a Captaine, and returne againe into Egipt.* If they haue not their mindes, the danger may bee, which in deede will bring some troubles that they are not vnlike to become either *Atheists* or *Papistes*.

Shortlie after the straunge attempt before mentioned that was made against the king of *Scotland*, Anno 1585, by ten thousand of his owne people at *Sterling:* (whereby the consistorian Ministers preuailed, aswell against their Soueraigne, as against their Bishops, for the aduancing of their presbiteries): there came out a rayling *Dialogue*, here in *England* published abroade in print and scattered by the brotherhoode, throughout the whole Realme.

This *Dialogue* is intituled: *the state of the church of England laid open in a conference, betweene Diotrephes* (representing the person of a Bishop,) *Tertullus a Papist*, (brought in to pleade for the orders of our church,) *Demetrius, a Vsurer* (signifying such as liue by vnlawful trades:) *Pandocheus, an Inkeeper,* (a receyuer of al, and a soother of euery ry man for his gaine:) and *Paule a preacher of the worde of God*: (sustayning the place and persons of the *Consistoriall* brethren.)

Where, (by the way,) see againe the account they make of all that do maintaine the present state of the Church: they are but *ambitious worldlings : Papistes : liuers by vnlawfull trades :* and *men pleasers.* But themselues are *Apostles*.

In this *Dialogue*, *Paule* is set forth as a man desirous, (vpon the *Innekeepers* motion,) to heare some good newes from *Scotland*: who meeting with the *Bishop*, hee vseth him according to the Consistorian humor: that is, most proudly, most spitefully, and most slaunderously. He condemneth both the calling of *Bishops* as *Antichristian*, and censureth al their proceedings, as wicked, Popish, vnlawfull, and cruell. He affirmeth that all the good, that hath beene done for the present flourishing estate of the Gospell in *England*: *hath* [a] *beene brought to passe, by those men, whom the Bishops despise, and by that course, which they were euer ennemies vnto.* a E. 1. *He saith, that* [b] *very many of all degrees, are fully perswaded in the matters of reformation, and that he is perswaded, this will come of it, vz. that he shall see the gouernement of the Church, (by the rules of their discipline) set vp before it be long.* b F. 1.

The Bishop is supposed to haue beene sent out of *England* into *Scotland*, for the suppressing of the *Presbiteries* there: and so is made, vpon his returne homewarde, to be the reporter of the *Scottish* affaires, and withall to signifie his great feare, least he and the rest of the *Bishops* in *England*, should bee serued shortly, as the *Bishops* had lately beene in *Scotland*, namely at *Edenburgh* and Sainct *Andrewes* &c.

Ah (saith the pretended *Bishop*) *my hoste. The Puritanes*

B.2. *in Scotland haue got-vp their discipline, and vtterly ouerthrown all the soueraignty of Bishops: by which they preuailed so mightily, that we feared, our fal in England shortlie to ensue. Whereupon I was sent, together with this my frend* (Tertullus,) *who came out of Fraunce into England: to goe and seeke the subuersion of their great assemblies, and the rest of their iurisdiction: wherein I preuailed a while, but now it is worse then euer it was. And it came so to passe: because the whole land cried for Discipline againe; and the Noble men so stifly did stand to it: and lastly the Ministers that came home from England, dealt so boldly with the king; that I was vtterly cast out, without all hope euer to doe any good there againe, and now I make homeward in hast, least I loose all there also.*

Here you haue the brethrens approbation of the aforsaide attempt in *Scotland*: whereby it is apparaunt, that if they shal be able to bring the people to such a kind of clamor, and the nobility to such a manner of stifnes: they can be wel content for their partes, to haue her maiestie vsed, as the *Scottish king* was: for it is according to their *Geneua* Diuinity.

F,2,& 3, &c. *Tertullus* the *Papist*, he is made the *Bishops* only Councellour, in the whole course of the gouernment of our Church: by whose aduise, (the author of the *Dialogue* saith) that the *Bishops* do beare with the Popish recusants, and that so many waies are sought to suppresse the Puritanes. This *Tertullus*, together with the *Host* and the *Vsurer*, do relate to the *Bishop* those occurrents in *Englande*, which had fallen out and hapned in his absence. And vppon the occasion of this question, asked by the *Bishop*: vz. *haue not the Bishops yet suppressed the Puritans, neither with countenance, nor by authority?* *Tertullus* maketh this aunswere. *Suppressed: no, my Lord: a friend of mine writte unto me, that one of their preachers saide in the Pulpit; he was per-*

perswaded that there were a 100000. of them in England, and that the number of them increased dayly in euery place, of all estates & degrees.

Is it not time for the Magistrates to looke about them? They do take it in scorne to bee thought so weake, as that they could bee suppressed. Bee it, they flatter themselues therein: yet their desire is apparant, that (if they be suffered, and shall euer be able) they will bring it to that passe. And if this be not a necessary consequent of the premisses: my iudgement faileth me. But to proceede.

Chap. II.

Of their doctrine for making a reformation themselues, and how the people must be thrust into that action.

ABout foure yeares since, it should seeme that some of the brethren, were of opinion, that they had dealt long inough in the practise of their Discipline, after such a secret manner: and that then they were bound in dutie to proceede to the publike exercise of it, notwithstanding any daunger, that might therby ensue. For thus one of them writeth. *Our zeale to Gods glorie, our loue to his Church, & the due planting of the same, in this horheaded age should be so warme & and stirring in vs, as not to care what aduenture we giue, and what censures we abide &c. The Iesuites & Seminaries, their diabolicall boldnes, will couer our faces with shame &c.* And after also in the same letter. *We cãnot be discharged, of great disloyalty to our cõming Christ, except we proceed* Payne to F.

 with

with practise, and so to further the Lords cause by suffering: forasmuch as that dutifull suffering, for so honorable a matter, is as sure a signe of subiection, as obeying, the time so vrging that bounden duetie. It is verily more then time, to Register the names of the fittest and hottest brethren round about our seuerall dwellings, whereby to put Maister Snecanus *godly counsell in execution: vz. Si quis obijciat &c. If any man obiect, that the setting vp, and the lawfull practise of the discipline in the Church, is hindred by the ciuill magistrate: let the magistrate bee freely and modestlie admonished of his duety. If he esteeme to be accounted, either a godly or a Christian magistrate, without doubt hee will admitte wholesome counsailes. But if he do not, yet let him bee more exactlie instructed, that he may serue God in feare, and bend his authority to the defence of the church and of Gods glory. Marry, if by this way there happen no good successe, then let the ministers of the Church, execute their office, according to the appointment of Christ. For they must rather obay God then men. In this last point, we haue dolefully failed, which now or neuer standeth vs in hand to prosecute with all celerity, without lingring and staying so long for Parliaments.*

This aduise of *Paines*, was thought by the brethren, (as I gesse) to be somewhat too rash. For of likelihoode they could not finde at that time, so sufficient a number of such *hotte brethren* as might serue their turne. Whereupon (as I suppose) out commeth the decrees of the *Warwick-shire Classes*, that for the increasing of the said number, *euery minister, (as occasion serued,) should teach the Discipline vnto the people, as wel as the other partes of the Gospel.* And for the moderating of *Paines* too hastie aduise, it was thus determined. *Non dum solicitandum esse publicè vniuersum cœtum ad praxim Disciplinæ, donec meliùs instituantur homines in eius cognitione:* that is: *As yet the whole multitude are not to be allured (publikely) to the practise of the Discipline, vntil men bee*

better

better instructed, in the knowledge of it. As though for the answering of *Payne*, they had said; that when by that means they had gotten, a sufficient number to assiste them, then his counsaile should be followed.

For you must vnderstand, that their chiefest trust is reposed in the people, as it may be further made more plain vnto you by the deposition of maister *Edmonds,* whose wordes I will set downe, as they remaine in record. *I doe well remember* (saith he) *that after I had left that company,* meaning the *London assemblies, meeting with Master* Field, *I talked with him, what harme was already done, by inueighing against the present state of the Church, and by their proceedings, in beating this their new reformation into the heades of the common people, because they were alreadie growen thereby amongest themselues, into great diuisions: very contemptuous, insolent, & intractable, &c, Whereunto hee answered, tush, holde your peace: seeing we cannot compasse these things, by suite nor dispute: it is the multitude and people, that must bring them to passe.* But I will leaue their endeuours a while, how they may seduce the people, and enter into a discourse of their further proceedings.

CHAP. III.

They would haue the nobility and the inferior Magistrates to set vp their discipline: & of their supplication with a 100000 hãds.

IT is here to be considered, what course they take, to bring the Nobility and inferior magistrates of *England*, to the beforesaid stifnes, (mentioned in the first Chapter) that was in them of *Scotlãd:* *Maister Penry* exhorteth the *Lord President of Wales*, by the examples of *Moses*

Suppl. to the gouern. of Wales. pa. 15. 16. 36. 37. 38. 39.

ses, Iehosuah, Dauid, Salomon, Iehosophat, Hezechiah, Iosue, Nehemiah, &c. & to take in hād their pretended reformation, in that countrie: prouing that he hath authority therunto, because hee *is a gouernour vnder God*, and that if hee refused so to doe; *he could haue no commission to rule there, in that therby Christ being reiected, he was become but the Lieutenant of Sathan.* Here you haue *Allobrogical*, and *Consistoriall* stuffe, able of it selfe, (if it were receiued) to fill all Christian kingdomes, with all kinde of mutinies, sedition, and rebellion. They would make the *inferior Magistrates, vnder their Soueraigne to beleeue*: that they had, (for their times, and *within their limittes*,) as absolute authority, as if they themselues were fully Princes there: and were not manie waies restrayned, by the supreme Magistrate. Surely if they shall bee able, by these and such like perswasions, to draw vnto them the *Iustices* of *Peace*, the *Shirifes* or *Lieutenants* of euery *Shire*, (and so make them the executioners of their good pleasures and platformes, without any further Commission or warrant from her Maiestie:) they shall not neede to expect eyther Prince, or Parliament, but may throwe downe and set vp, as greate builders doe, whatsoeuer shall be most agreeable, to the mutabilitie of their owne affections.

Goodman with the consent of the Geneuians &c p. 214. 215

And whereas an obiection might haue beene made, that if either the Noblemen, Gentlemen, or people shold take vpon them to cast downe the *Bishops*, and to reforme the church, according to their raigning frēzy, without her maiesties commandement, that in so doing they shold greatly disturbe the state of the Realme, and highly offēd her most excellent maiestie: these points are both of them passed ouer with a snuffe, & with great disdaine, as being no such impediments, as ought to hinder the valiant corages

rages of *Consistorian* subiects. *I tell you true*, (saith one of their Captaines) *I thinke it a greate blessing of God, that hath raised vp* Martin *to hold tackling with the* Bishops, *that you may haue some time of breathing, or rather a time to gather courage and zeale, &c. to set vppon these ennemies, &c. For if, as hitherto you haue, you bee so loth, for disturbing of our state, forsooth and the offending of her Maiestie, not onelie to speak against but euen vtterlie to reiect this* Hierarchy *of our Bishops, euen to haue no more to doe with it, then with the* seate *of the* beast: *you shall declare vnto our children, that God can set vp, but a company of whiteliuered souldiers &c.* Forsooth if this exhortation be according to their Discipline: it ought no longer to be tearmed Christs, (as they tearme it) but the Diuels Discipline. And yet, because they would not haue her Maiestie altogether neglected, an other of their *Lieutennants* can be content, that (before their souldiers mentioned, shoulde beginne the skirmish) there might bee first, (as it were) for a parlee, some little ouuerture of duetie signified: that, if (as yet) her Highnesse woulde bee ruled by them, they would desist. To this purpose hee moueth all the *Puritanes*, (as hee tearmeth them,) in *England* both Lordes, Knightes, Gentlemen, Ministers and people, to offer a supplication to her Maiestie: in effect, for the full obtayning of all their desires.

Martin Iun. Epilog.

Martin sen.

To this (saith he) an hundred thousand hands would be gotten &c. and then *thou* (speaking to his reader) *may well thinke, what a stroke so many would strike together, &c. It should appeare, that they are not few, and of small reputation, but in a manner the strength of our land, and the sinow of her Maiesties royal gouernment, which our Bishops do falsely note with the names of Puritanes, The consideration whereof, I tell thee, euen in policie, would make, that this their suite should not bee ha-*

* T *stily*

stily reiected, especially in such a time, as wherein we now liue, in daunger of our enemies abroad, and therefore had need of no causes of discouragement at home. I like it well when men will deale plainelie, You see indeede their hearts. And is it not then euident, whereat they ayme? *In such a time no pollicy?* Indeede the returne of the *Spaniard* was then expected. No neede then of discouragement at home? Why? wanting your desires, wold you haue taken no part, if the *Spaniard* had come? or purposed you, to haue made a more readie passage for him, by rebelling at home, before he should haue come? or would you haue ioyned with him, if he had come? or meant you thereby, (through terror) to haue enforced her Maiestie, to your purposes, least you should haue taken some of these courses? Chose which of them you list: the best is seditious.

Chap. IIII.

Presuming vpon some vnlawful assistance, they vse very violent wordes.

Ow true it is, that they haue a hundreth thousand, ready at their direction, I know not: but they haue surely too many: if the companion of the brotherhood, that sent his humble motion abroade, may be herein beleeued. *Thousands* (he saith) *do sigh for this discipline, and ten thousand haue sought it: and approued and worthy men of euery shire, haue consented vnto it.*

pag. 39

But certaine it is such is their hope, to thrust the people, with the rest of their confederates, into some vnlawfull execution, of their distempered designementes: that they

are

are come to a wonderfull resolution and assurance, as hauing almost (in their own conceipts,) obteined alreadie, the verie scepter of their kingdome. *The Eldershippe is at hande*, (saith the *humble motioner*.) And againe: vsing reasons, why the state here in *England* shoulde presentlie embrace their gouernement, hee falleth vpon these two pointes, (iumping iustlie, with the *Scottish* ministers logique, mentioned before by *Diotrephes*, the pretended *Bishop*,) vz. *the people are inflamed with zeale*, and (as it seemeth) the second reason dependeth vpon the first: that is, *because it is harde, daungerous, and impossible to stand against it*. In effect, the people crie for the *Discipline*, and therefore it must needes preuaile. Indeede they haue slaunderously set out supplications and complaints in the name of the comminaltie: thereby to terrifie their withstanders. But I trust the people generally are not so madde, although there bee some that are straungely bewitched: vnto this conceipt of the peoples readines it seemeth to mee, that *M. Snape* had relation, when hee vsed these wordes following, as they are set down by the othes of some of them, to whom he spake them. *How say you* (quoth hee) *if we* meaning himselfe and his fellow ministers, with their adherentes *deuise a way, whereby to shake off all the Antichristian yoake, and gouernment of the Bishops: & will iontly together erect the discipline and gouernment all in one day: but peraduenture it wil not be yet, this yeare & a halfe*.. An other, (of his more then superabundant charitie) foreseeing the mischiefes that are ready to fal by his brethrens procurement, vpon the Bishops of this realme: giueth them warning to be gone in time. *Bee packing Bishops*, (saith he) *you striue in vaine: you are laid open alreadie*.

Holmes, Hawgar. &c.

Epistle to mart. epitome.

Friers and Monkes were not so bad. Looke to your selues: for my sonnes will not see their father thus persecuted at your hands.

W.F.

handes. *We protest* (say the authors of a certaine supplication, drawen to her Maiesty: and found in one of the brethrens studies: but he wil not confesse, by whose aduise it was penned:) *We protest* (say they) *vnto your Maiestie: that we will be no longer subiect vnto the Bishops vnlawfull and vsurped authority &c. Wherefore let them not looke for it at our handes.* And an other. *The trueth will preuaile* (speaking of the discipline) *in spight of your teeth* (meaning the Bishops,) *and all other aduersaries of it.* Likewise an other dealeth as charitably with the common wealth, as his fellow did with the *Bishops*: that is: he warneth to take heede: saying, *that it will be very dangerous to our state, to mayntaine two contrary factions: that the Magistrates are then bound, euen for the quieting of our state, to put downe the one: that those, that stande for the discipline, neither can nor will giue it ouer, (so as they will not bee put downe): and that the saide Magistrates cannot maintayne the corruption of our Church, namely Archbishops and Bishops, without the discontentment of their subiectes.*

Epistle to the Demonst.

Martin iun. Thes, 98. 103. 100, 105.

And an other: *we haue sought to aduance this cause of God, by humble suite to the Parliament, by supplication to your* Conuocation *house, by wrighting in defence of it, and by challenging to dispute for it: seeing none of these meanes vsed by vs haue preuayled: if it come in by that meanes, which will make all your harts to ake, blame your selues.*

Martins protestation.

And to conclude. *In this one point* (saith another) *the Bishops are of my minde: vz. that reformation cannot well come to our Church, without bloud.* Let the place be througly considered. The wordes are ambiguously set downe: of purpose to couer (in some sort) the crueltie, which lurketh in their own heartes. For in my simple iudgement, his speaches can haue no other good & coherent sence, then this, vz. that as the Bishops do think (as he slaunderously deemeth

meth) that there can be no reformation of the *Puritanes* disordered proceedings, without the bloud of some of their brotherhoode, so he is of minde, that the reformatiō which he and his companions do seeke for, cannot be attained vnto, without the bloud of some of those, that doe withstand their platformes. It is true that hee there onely prosecuteth the cruel opinion, which hee ascribeth to the *Bishops*: saying that *no bloud can handsomly be spilt, vnlesse they be the butchers*. But he passeth cunningly by his own mind, as very wel knowing his companions capacities. Indeed, if they do take vpon them to spil bloud, they cannot (thanks be to God) as yet, do it handsomely. The Lord of his infinite mercy graunt that their opportunities, to such a mischief, do neuer serue them better, then hitherto they haue done.

CHAP. V.

Vpon Cartwrights committing to prison: some strange attempts were looked.

BEsides, prayers to preuent such outrages (as are mentioned in former chapters) there must be other meanes diligently looked into. For out of question, it is high time. Euery one is acquainted with the execution of *Hack*. but few do vnderstand, the secretes of those attempts. They stretch much further then they are supposed.

You may remember, the *Disciplinarie* mens doctrine (before mentioned) vz. that when Princes grow to be tyrants, (whereof seditious spirites will be the iudges, (and that the inferiour Magistrates will not do their duties: the people then, (if any *Ionathan* will step foorth, to be their captaine) are bound to ioyne themselues vnto him, and

Buch, de iure regn. 57. Goodman. pag. 185. Iunius Brutu s. 170. Beza de authorit. magist. in subd. p. 97

 may

I.P. Of obedience. Whittinghams preface Goodman pag.196, I.P.121.

may vse the sword in their own right: or otherwise some priuate man,that is moued with zeale *extra ordinem*, may execute vengeance, vppon prince or Potentate, Idolater, wicked persons,&c.euen as the spirit shal moue him. The which doctrine(as I said)they take vpon them to cōfirm, out of the scriptures:by these examples vz.of *Phineas*,who in zeale killed the adulterers:of *Ahud*, who in zeale killed king *Eglon*, in his priuate chamber: of *Iaell*, who in zeale killed *Sisara*: of *Matathias*, who in zeale killed a *Iew*, for committing Idolatrie: and of the same *Matathias*, who in the same zeal killed likewise,at the same time,the kings commissioners,that commanded the people to conform themselues to the kings proceedings.&c.

To those that know these principles,how can it be eyther obscure or difficult,what they are both to thinke & iudge,when they shall heare of any *extraordinary* callings, and secret motions,in priuate men: whereby they shall take vpon them, (through the assistance of giddy & seduced malecontentes,) to correct and amend, to set vp and throw downe,to deliuer and restraine,to punish and execute,how,what,where,when and whom,&c. according to their own pleasures:and all vnder pretence of such directions, as they shall affirme that the holy Ghost doth minister vnto them.

Vpon the proceedings, held by course of law,against *Vdall* and some others:and likewise by reason, that certaine Preachers, but especiallie maister *Cartwright*, being called before her Maiesties commissioners in causes ecclesiastical,for their aforesaide vndutyfull proceedings,were (vpon iust occasions)committed to prison : the matter was greatly grudged at, & so taken to heart,amongst the reforming and zealous brotherhoode,as that many deuises and complots,were(as it seemeth)in deliberation not

onely

onely how the saide prisoners, might (for the present) bee defended and deliuered: but also how thereupon they might proceede, for the setting vp of their Discipline. To this purpose, in mine opinion these words of *Wiggintons* are verie pertinent. *Maister Cartwright is in the Fleete, for refusall of the othe (as I heare) and Maister Knewstubs is sent for, and sondry worthy ministers are disquieted, who haue been spared long. So that wee looke for some bickering ere long, and then a battel: which cannot long endure.* How far these wordes may bee drawne, I leaue it to be considered of, by those that can discerne of such like kind of phrases. This I can assure you of, that (vppon what grounds I know not) through the course which was held by the magistrats here, against the said prisoners: there was great expectation, and as it were a hope conceiued by their fauorers, in another cuntrey, of some bickering amongst vs, (about that time,) as *Wigginton* writeth of. Thus a man that hath been of especiall account in *Scotland*, did write vnto a friend of his in *England. I attend your next answere, aswell of the estate of your Church, as of all other affaires. For there is here great worde of sondry vprores, which I trust be false, or repressed in due season by her Maiestie.*

Wigginton, to Porter at Lancaster, 6. Nouemb. 1590.

P.A, 7. Decemb. 1590.

But that passeth all (to this purpose,) which falleth out most apparantlie, by the view taken of such letters and papers, as were found vpon the apprehension of *Hacket* and his Prophets.

Chap. VI.

One Edmond Copinger tooke vpon him to worke Cartwrightes &c. deliuerance: he pretendeth an extraordinary calling and acquainteth diuers with it: one Gibson a Scot: P. Wentwotrh, Cartwright, Wigginton, Charke, Trauers, Egerton, &c.

Whilest

Hilest some were deuising of one way, and some of an other, for the good of the saide prisoners, &c. One *Edmond Coppinger*, with his familiars, could find no meanes to bee looked for, except it might please God, according to the foresaide positions, to stir vp some zealous brethren, by some extraordinary calling, to effect their desires. This cogitation (as it seemeth) no soner grew vpon thē, but that by and by they fealt, (as they thought) in themselues: some certaine slender instigations, to such a heauenly purpose. It appeareth that towards the latter end of *December*, 1590. *Copinger*, *Arthington*, and *Iohn Bentley*, [a] maister *Knightlies* man, did hold a fast, at one *Thomas Lancasters* house, a scholemaister in *Shoe-lane*. It began vpon the *Saturday* at night, and held till *Sonday* at night. In the time of this fast, vz. the *Saterday* [b] at night, *Coppinger* (as he said) found himself *very extraordinarily exercised &c. with a wonderfull zeale, to set forth Gods glory any waies, which lawfully he might enter into.* At that time also, (I mean at that last fast: *Arthington had likewise his extraordinary calling*. Thus *Copinger* did write of his matter to *Lancaster*: the letter was also subscribed vnto, by *Arthington*. *In* [c] *your house, in your presence, and partly by your meanes; I had my first extraordinarie calling, and of the same minde is my brother Arthington.* *Copinger* the next day after the saide fast, did ride into *Kent*: and vpon his returne, (which was with some speed) he signified vnto his fellow-fasters, how he had been extraordinarily called, both before his going, the said *Satterday at night*: & also in his iourney, since he departed from them: vz. how God had *reuealed* [d] vnto him, such a secret mystery, as was wonderful. *By the way* (saith he) *as I rid, I fansied to my selfe, that there was leaue giuen mee, to speake to God*

a Coppinger examined, 19 of Iuly. Arthing. discourse.

b Coppinger to T.C.

c Coppinger and Arthing. to Lancaster, the 15. of Iuly 1591.

d Arthing, discourse.

Cop. to T.C.

God, in a more familiar manner, then at any time before: also I perswaded my self, that his spirite did giue me many straunge directions, wherein the Lord would vse me to doe seruice to his most glorious Maiestie, and to his Church. Concerning the substance of his said reuelation, hee also tolde, *Arthington* & *Lancaster* thus much: vz. *that he knew a way, how to bring the Queene to repentance, and to cause all her Counsell and Nobles, to do the like, out of hand, or els detect them, to bee traytors that refused.* Arthingtons discourse.

After the relation of these things, within a day or two, this *Copinger* and *Arthington*, held another fast by themselues. *Whereupon* (saith *Copinger*) *I was againe stirred vp, to such businesse of such importance, as in the eyes of flesh and bloud, was likelie to bring much danger to my selfe, and vnlikely to bring any good successe to the Church of God.* Cop. to T, C.

Of these his instigations, or reuelations, hee writ *to some preachers in the Realme: and to some without*: as namelie a letter the last day of December, 1590. to one *Gibson*, a kinde of preacher in *Scotland*. Wherein hee greatly complayneth of the present state of our Church: and desireth of him, to bee instructed from the brethren there, in diuers points, concerning an extraordinarie calling. *Thee state of our Church* (saith hee) *groweth worse and worse: our zealous Ministerie and Magistracie are daylye disgraced and displaced: the meanes of helpe is taken away, except, that God woulde eyther moue her Maiestie inwardly, shee being bereaued of those holy helpes, which Gods seruantes enioy in the publike exercise of religion: or else stirre vp, some faithfull* Zorobabell *or* Nehemiah, *to let her see how the Lordes house lyeth waste, and how vsurpers of Antichristian tiranny, doe keepe Christ Iesus from gouerning in his kingdome.* And then hee addeth. *My selfe am acquainted with some, who, to do seruice herein, would aduenture the losse of their liues, so that* Cop to T.C. Copping to Gibson.

they might haue warrant from the worde, for their so doing, and haue approbation by the Church. And to this end they fancy to themselues to haue receiued an extraordinary calling, wherein they feare to be abused by Sathan. Then followeth his petitiō. *And therefore I, thogh most vnworthy, haue aduentured to write vnto you, to beseech you in the bowels of Christ Iesus, to haue conference with such, as are most able to aduise you on our behalfe, and to returne answere, how a man may examine himselfe in this matter, and what be the extraordinarie thinges, which must bee in him, that is so called: what course he is to take, to haue his extraordinarie calling knowne: first to himselfe, and then to the Church.*

After hee had sent away this letter into *Scotland* hee began to draw his doubts into some Methode: and did propound them all in eight questions. The chiefe summe whereof, is this, *whether in these dayes, and in this countrey, where there is but preaching heere and there, where the Discipline is not established, but oppugned, by the publike Magistrates, whether there bee place for any extraordinarie calling, immediately from God, of workers and helpers to his Church &c.* These questions thus contriued hee sent them to his olde acquaintance *Wigginton:* who iustly according to *Copingers* humor, aunswered them all affirmatiuely: as his aunswers are to be shewed, vnder his owne hand, and as *Copinger* did also write vnto maister *Cartwright*; the effect of which Letter will follow in course.

Vpon *Copingers* receite of this aunswere, that there was high time, for such extraordinary callings: *presently after, therwas an other fast procured by Copinger*, for a better cōformation of such his manner of calling, and to see, if any mo might be drawn thereby into the same conceipt. *This fast was held vppon the Wednesday, in a Marchauntes house, where*

Cop. to T. C.

where Wigginton then lay, and Wigginton himselfe with three or fower others was present at it. But before this fast was held, *meanes was vsed* (saith *Copinger*) *to haue some notice giuen to some of the Preachers in Prison, of the day of their humiliation, and of their desire to haue them commend vnto God in their praiers the holy purposes, which any fearing God, should in time attempt to take in hand, by seeking the glorie of God, and the good of the Church.* Cop. exam. 19.Iulie. Cop. to T.C.

The effect of their prayers in this fast, was this, vz. *They humbly beseech Almighty God, that if hee had appointed to vse any of them, to doe any special seruice to him and his: and that to that end would extraordinarily call them, that he would seale vp his or their so calling by some special manner, and by his holy spirite, and giue such extraordinarie graces and giftes, as were fitte for so waightie an action.* Copin exam. 19.Iulie. Cop to T.C.

How the rest of this company sped hereby, I finde it not: but *Copinger* (as hee sayth) *was called againe the same night in a dreame*. The manner whereof, he thus describeth. *About the midde part of the night, I thought my selfe in my sleepe, to be carried into Heauen, and there being wonderfullie astonished with the Maiestie of God, and brightnes of his glorie, I made a lowde and most strong noice &c. since which time, I find euery day more & more comfort: and suppose, there is somwhat in me &c. to worke* (he meaneth some strange reformation.) Copin. exam. Cop. to T.C.

As before it hath bene partly touched, *Copinger* did not only craue the aduise of some ministers in these his great actions, (as oft he tearmed them): but also of such of the Laity, as he thought were most fitte to ioine with him, or to aduise him: and I doubt not, but that he dealt as plainly with them, as he had done before with *Dauison* a *Scotte* and others. This doth appeare in some sort, by a Letter written vnto *Copinger* by *Peter Wentworth*, the fiue and twentith of Ianuarie 1590. in answere of one sent vnto him before, from *Copinger*. It seemeth that *Copinger* ha-

P.W. to Cop. 25. Ian, 1590. uing desired maister *Wentworth* to come vnto him to *London*, that they might conferre together, &c. for answere he excuseth himselfe in respect of his lamenes. &c. and *of his debillitie and weakenes, to giue aduise in matters of importance, wherein I perceiue* (saith hee) *you are labouring*. And further (saith hee,) *I do assure my selfe, that the purpose tendeth vnto the true seruice of God, and of her Maiestie. I beseech you resort to the Lorde, to direct your labours both in matter and manner. For an ill manner may marre a good matter. You are in a plentiful soile, where you may vse the aduise of many godly wise. Vse the benefite thereof, and then as* Iosuah saide, *bee bolde, and of good courage: feare not to bee discouraged.*

Besides it appeareth by a Letter of *Copingers* to *Thomas*

Cop. to L. 29. Ian. 15. 19 *Lancaster*, the scholemaister, dated the nine and twentith of *Ianuarie*: that he had disclosed, (as it should seeme, all the premises, vnto diuerse of the Ministers of *London*, desiring to haue had *some conference with them*: and offering himselfe to be *directed either to proceede, or draw backe, as the Church should aduise*. But they supposing the *matter to bee too harde to bee effected: and him an vnfitte man to manage it*, refused to admitte of any such conference. In the same letter, it is also euident, that *Copinger* had made *the night before a rude discourse* (as he tearmeth it) to *Lancaster* of these matters, which *Lancaster* disliked. And touching some speeches had with maister *Egerton*, thus he there writeth. *Most true it is, that he refused to take triall of mee, and of my giftes: alledging, that he was a meane ordinarie man &c. and one that could not iudge of extraordinary giftes: and withall, most Christianly, wisely, and louinglie perswaded me, to be carefull & circumspect ouer my selfe: to take heede least I was deceiued by the*

subtil-

subtilitie of Sathan, and so misse-led: whereby I might endanger my selfe, both for my liberty, estate, and credit, and also bee an hinderance to the great cause, which I would seeme to be most desirous to further. But withall he concluded, that he would bee loath, to quench the spirite of God in mee, or to hinder my zeale.

In another letter also, to the said *Lancaster* from *Copinger*: concerning other his proceedings with *Egerton*, he saith: *it cannot bee denied, but that the cause is good, which I desire to be an actor in: but it is saide by some, that it is impossible that I should be fit to meddle therein.* He also desireth *Lancaster*, to deal with *Egerton*, that he might haue *a sight of al the letters, which he* (the said *Copinger*) *had written vnto him about these matters.*

About this time it also appeareth, that *Copinger* fell into some dealings with *M. Cartwright*, concerning the premises: and that he had sent vnto him, the questions before mentioned, for to know his resolution, whether it would be agreeable to *Wigintons*. He writ a letter vnto him, dated the 4. of February 1590. beginning thus.

Right reuerend Sir, your most wise and christian councell, together with offer to take knowledge by writing frō me, of such matters, as might induce me to suppose my selfe, to haue receiued some hope of speciall fauor from god, to some special vse: doth moue me more and more to admire his mercies towardes mee &c. In this letter, he signifieth to *M. Cartwright* (as before I haue noted,) the number of their fastes, his seuerall callings, his writinge to some preachers within the Realme, and to some without: and his confirmation by *Wigintons* said answeres, and maketh these petitions vnto him: vz. *that the church* (*I meane*, saith he, *your selfe & such as you shal name vnto me:*) *would look narrowly into him, for the trial of his extraordinary calling. If* (saith he) *I be thought to be any wayes miss-led,*

I craue sharpe censuring: If I be guided by Gods spirit to any good end, (as heareafter shall be adiudged,) I shal be ready to acquaint you and them, with generalities and particularities, so far-foorth as you and they be desirous to looke into them. And his second petition was, vz. *to haue* (saith hee) *your further answere to some questions, wherein I desire to be resolued: with your direction also, what hereafter I am to signifie to your selfe, concerning the matter it selfe.*

After M. *Cartwright* had receaued this letter from *Copinger*, he sent vnto him a message, *that he should attempt nothing but by aduise, and that he should be wise and circumspect.* Besides it seemeth, that vpõ *Copingers* so earnest sute made as hath bene specified, there was a time appointed, that he might be conferred withall. These things do appeare to be true, by a second letter of *Coppingers* to *Cartwright*, the *13.* of February. Wherin he greatly complaned that *he had beene put backe from that seruice of god and his church, which he had in hand, (and that by his frends:) he desired M. Cartwright that the day appointed for conference might holde*, and hee addeth this reason. *The daunger which some stand in: for their liues, is not vnknowne: and if I had not beene letted, I durst haue ventured my life, to haue procured their release ere now.*

Copinger to T. C. 13. of febr. 1590.

And againe to the same effect. *As I may, I command you in the name of God, that you aduise the preachers, to deale speedely and circumspectlie, least some bloode of the Saintes be shed.* In the ende hee signifieth, that the next day, hee with some others, *did meane to humble themselues in fasting, and that the prisoners did know of it.*

Whilest *Copinger* was in expectation of the said conference: how it fel out I know not, but (as it seemeth) councel was taken, & the matter ouer-ruled, that the ministers appointed, should vtterly refuse to haue any conference

with

with him. Wherupon *M. Cartwright, Trauers, Charke,* and *Egerton*, sent him worde by M. *Hockenhull, that they would leaue him, to himselfe: or rather to Sathan: and that they thought him vnworthy, to bee conferred withall.* And this appeareth by *Coppingers* letter to *Charke, Trauers* & *Egerton* beginning thus: *Right reuerend fathers &c.* About the deliuery of this message, *Copinger* did after, (in some sort) chalenge *M. Hockenhull*: and told him also, *that seeing he had beene refused to bee conferred with-all, by those godly, wise, and zealous preachers, who hadde promised to haue had conference with him &c. occasion therby was offered vnto him, to approue himselfe.* Coppinger to Charke, Trauers and Egerton. Cop to Hockenh. 24. Feb 1590.

About this time or a little before, *Coppinger* receiued a letter in answere of his, from *Gibson* (the Scottish Minister aboue mentioned:) dated from *Pententland* in *Scotland* the sixt of Februarie 1590. concerning the pointes of *Coppingers* saide letter vnto him. Wherein hee writeth very cunningly, touching *Coppingers* question, and shifteth it ouer (like his craftes-maister) with an indirect and vncertaine aunswere. But in these pointes hee is very plaine: vz. that hee *had shewed Coppingers letter to sundrie: that hee had conferred of it with the best of their Ministerie: that their Church was not forgetful to do al good offices, for the weale of the brethren here: that there was a writing ready to send to* Germany *to* Iunius, *that he would trauaile with some of the good & wel affected professors there: that (of his knowledge) trauaile was to be made with some others, as namely the* King *of* France *and that their ministery would themselues trauaile with her Maiestie.* No doubt if *Iunius* or any other, at their request shall take vpon them, to deale with her highnesse, for men of *Coppingers* humor or for any of those, whom he would haue deliuered, the suggestions (which either are, or must be made vnto them,) are like to containe many slaunders and vntruthes. But to goe forward.

Chap. VII.

How Coppinger and Arthington came acquainted with Hacket: of their conference with Io. Throg. Coppingers letter to Io. Throg. and his answere.

Hacket to Wigginton 3. march, 1590.

Hortly after this time, vz. the 3. of March 1590. *William Hacket*, an olde companion of *Wigintōs* did write vnto him, and doth comfort him then in prison, with the exāples of *Gideons empty pitchars*, of the deliuerance *by Moses through the red sea*, and of *Haman that was hanged vpon the same gibbet, he had prepared for an other*. Hee vseth also these words. *Master Wigginton: I desire to communicate my spirite at large with you: but I know not your keeper &c. Good M.* Wigginton, *make my sound heart, knowen to M.* Cartwright, *M.* Snape, *M.* Vdall, *M.* Lord.

Hackets discourse.

In the *Easter* terme, this *Hacket* came vp to London, of likelyhood to communicate his spirite with *Wigginton*, & to grow into acquaintnance with the parties named: but his pretence was, *partly to see what would become of Iob, Throgmorton, and partlie to reckon with Wigginton, about the making of malt betweene them together.* He had not beene long *in London*, but hee came to *Wigginton*, who (amongst other discourses) tolde *Hacket* that there was a *Gentlman (meaning M. Coppinger) in the Cittie, a very good man &c.* He describeth him vnto *Hacket, and the matter also hee was entring into*: signifiyng further, how *Coppinger had beene wonderfully discouraged* (in his purposes) *by the Preachers in*

London

London: but that hee (for his part) *had not so done. &c.* Hee also commended *Arthington* to *Hacket*, to be an honest man. Then *Wigginton sent for Copinger, and by Gods prouidence he came foorthwith vnto him : and M. Wigginton willed Copinger and Hacket, to take acquaintance one of the other: assuring Coppinger, that he knew Hacket to be a man truelie fearing God, and such a person, as God might minister some comfort to Copinger by his conference: that Hacket had beene tormented, and that for the* [a] *credite of Hackets suffrings, a hundreth could witnes.* About this time also, *Arthington by Wiggintons and Coppingers meanes (as hee sayth) fell into acquaintance with Hacket, meeting first with him at Mistris Lawsons house, M. Iob Throgmorton* also being the at *London*, grew into some conference (as it should seeme) with these three companions, *Coppinger*, *Arthington*, and *Hacket*. And this is gathered by *Coppingers* letter to *Iob Throgmorton*, after his departure from *London*, that tearme : and by the answere, returned from him vnder his owne hand, and sealed with his seale of armes. Both the letters are fit to be considered. Thus *Coppinger* writ vnto him, as it appeareth vnder his owne hand.

Arthing. ex 19. Iulie 1591.

Arthingt. ex 30. of Iuly 1591.

Arthingt. ex 19. of Iuly 1591.

My owne deare brother : my selfe and my two brethren, who lately were together with you in Knight-rider street, do much desire conference with you, which will aske some time. The busines is the Lords own, and he doth deale in it himselfe, in a strange and extraordinarie manner, in poore and simple creatures Much is done since you see vs, which you wil reioyce to heare of, when we shal meete: and therefore I beseech you, as soone as you receiue this letter, hasten an answere in writing, to my syster Randolphes house, at S. Peters hill foote, by Poules wharfe. Therin aduertise (I beseech you) when I may come to speake with you: for delayes are daungerous, and some of the great enemies begin to be so pursued

Where Hacket then lay by Coppingers appointment.

sued by God, as they are at their wits end. The Lorde make vs thankefull for it, who keepe vs euer to himselfe, to do his will and not ours.

Your very louing brother in the L. most aßured to command.

This coppie remaineth thus endorsed. *The coppie of a letter to M. Iob Throgmorton, from E. C.* And now followeth *Throgmortons* letter, beeing an answere (*as I take it*) *vnto Coppingers.*

My good brother, &c. (I reioyce that you will vouchsafe so to account of mee.) Your godlie conference at anie time, when oportunitie shall serue, I will not refuse. And albeit our busines may hinder vs now to meet, yet there is no time ouer past, but that it may be performed, when it please God. The next terme, (you heare) I must appeare here againe vppon my band: at which time you shall find, that I will be glad of your christian conference, or of any other brothers, by whom I may be enlightened. Lord deliuer mee, from that pride of heart, to reiect or refuse that while I liue. That course you speake of, intended by you, I was neuer (you know) in particular acquainted with. And therefore, for mee to like or dislike a matter, that I had no knowledge of, had beene (I take it) without ground or warrant. Onlie I confesse, I heard some buzzes abroad, of a sole and singular course, that either you, or some other had plotted in his head, which was greatly feared, and condemned of the brethren. What that was, as I know not, so had I small reason to speake of it with preiudice. Onelie I would wish you, and all that beare good will to the holie cause, in this perilous age of ours, to take both your eyes in your handes, (as they saie) and to be sure of your ground and warrant, before you striue to put in exeecution. For as I like not of coldnes of Zeale, vnder colour of discretion: so on the other side, I think that this sentence

of

of our sauiour (be ye wise as serpents) was not written in vain neither, and had great neede to be practised of some in this age. A sanctified cause, (you know) would alwayes haue a sanctified course. Our rule and square, must be the word of truth, which so long as we lay before vs, as our leuel, we shall not lightly swarue much from the marke. The Lord therefore direct vs, in these feareful and miserable daies, and let not our infirmities be a barre to his mercies. I know, (my good Brother,) that the greatest workes of the Lord: are wrought by the weakest instruments, least men should boast in the arme of flesh. And therefore, (were it not for my sinnes and vnworthynes,) I could easilie perswade my selfe, in regarde of my weaknes, that the Lord might effect something by me, who am priuy to mine owne wants, and farre short of those good giftes, it pleaseth you (of your loue) to loade mee with. But this worke, that you speake of, (howsoeuer the instrument bee compassed with weaknes,) must sure be wrought by a more sanctified heart, then my selfe can yet without hypocrisie boast of. And therefore, though in affection and good will I ioyne, yet I resigne the honor of the worke, to those, that the Lord hath more enabled. The man you speake of, (if he be at Oundhell,) dwelleth hard by a Sister of mine, and thereupon I shall haue the better occasion to see him, when it please God. Forget mee not in your holy praiers and meditations, and salute good Giles with many thankes, whose debtor I am in the Lord. Blessing vpon Syon: confusion vpon Babell. hast this 18. of the 5. Moneth.

Euer yours in the Lord.

Chap. VIII.

Copinger to Hacket of an appearance in the Starre-chamber: his letter to Vdall: why Cartwright, &c: refused to conferre with him: Cartwright resolued some questions of Coppingers: of eight preachers that did fast and pray for Coppingers successe.

AFter some few dayes, that *Hacket* had taried in *London*, the said Easter termẽ, he returned home againe to *Oundle*: hauing first promised *Coppinger*, that he would come vp againe vnto him, whensoeuer he sent for him. Nowe *Coppinger*, by his said conferences and acquaintance with *Hacket*, was grown (as he said) *very bold and couragious*. But yet shortly after, vz, (as I thinke) the seuenteenth of *May*, he liked so well of *Hackets* company, that he sent for him againe, to come vp vnto him: saying, *If Gods spirit direct you to come, come: if not, stay. But write with all speed, and conuey your letter, and inclose it in a letter to him, who brought you and me acquainted:* (that was *Wigginton*): *put not too your name, for discouery, &c*. And in the same letter, hee sendeth *Hacket* this newes. *The zealous Preachers (as it is thought) are to be in the Star-chamber to morrow.* (I thinke, he meaneth the last day of Easter tearme last.) *The L. by his holy spirit be with them, and stay all euill that is intended against them. My selfe, if I can get in, am moued to be there: and I feare, if sentence with seueritie shall be giuen, I shall be forced in the name of the great and fearefull God of heauen and earth, to protest against it.* About this time also, he writ a verie couragious letter to *Vdall* in prison: (for he confesseth it was written

Copinger to Hacket.

Copinger to Hacket. 17. of May. 1591.

written about tenne weekes, before his examination: which was the nineteenth of *Iuly*). In this letter he telleth him, that (*notwithstanding some brethrens hard opinions of him, and other discouragementes*) *yet now the Lord hath not onelie enabled him to fight, but at the length (in some sort, to vanquish and ouercome.* He signifieth allso vnto him, that *the next day, there were some few, that purposed to ioyne together, in a holy fast, in regard of the afflicted Saintes in generall, &c.* He greatly *commendeth the Ministers cause and suffringes, that are in prison, assuring himselfe that God will blesse all the actions in it.* He saith, there were diuerse *out of prison, lying hid, that in this great worke were hammering their heads, bestowing their braines, and spending their spirites: who doe hope (in short tyme) to be brought forth into the sight of their and your enemies, to defend the cause you stand for: whose presence (God assisting them,) will daunt the enemies more then yours: for that they be men voyde of learning, wisedome, and gifts, such as can challenge nothing to themselues, but must giue all to God: who in all the greatest workes, that euer haue beene wrought, hath vsed the weakest meanes, least men should boast in the arme of flesh. And therefore (I beseeche you) cheare vp your selues in the Lord: for the day of our redemption is at hand: and pray, that the hand of the Lord, may be strengthened in them, whom he hath appointed to take part with you in this cause.*

Copinger to Vdall. May 1591.

Hacket and his fellowes.

Here (you see) he was growne to a wonderfull resolution. But yet there is another letter of his, that wil make the same more euident, and likewise lay open more plainelie, some of the premises, then hitherto they haue beene. Hee sheweth therein, that hee could be still well contented, *to haue some conference with Maister Charke, Maister Trauers, Maister Egerton, Maister Gardiner, Maister Philips, and Maister Cooper.* But (sayth he) *I make not this suite, for that I would seeke to haue approbation from them, or any other liuing creature,*

The Copy of Cop. letter to a friend 21 May. 1591.

Creature, but from God himselfe.

You haue heard before, how these Ministers haue refused to confer with *Coppinger*. And what shoulde a man thinke, the cause might be? Surelie a feare they had: least he shoulde (by entring into some particulars) bring them, within the compasse of his dangerous complots. This may be necessarily there also gathered, in that as shewing hee could be content, to conferre with the said parties, not because (he protesteth) that he would seeke any approbation from them: so doth he likewise remou that doubt, saying, that *he purposed not to acquaint them with the courses, which he purposed, by Gods assistance, to take in hand, whereby great daunger might growe to them, and little good to him: but that they might be witnesses of his humilitie, &c.*

You haue heard also, of one of *Copingers* petitions to Maister *Cartwright*, for his aunswere to those questions mentioned, that he had before propounded to *Wigginton*. Whereunto it should seeme, that (although at the first he misliked that motion) yet in the end he yeelded. *My humble desire to you is* (sayth *Coppinger*) *that you (in my name) giue great thankes to good Maister Cartwright, for satisfying mee in some questions, which, at the first, he thought little vse to be made of.* Likewise it also appeareth, that Maister *Hockenhull* did his aforesaid message vnto *Copinger*, from the preachers, in harder manner then he had Commission. *For* (sayth he) *his counsaile*, (that is *Cartwrights*) *and cariage of himselfe, the Lord did direct and blesse it vnto mee: though the Messenger &c. in his cariage of himselfe, failed somewhat, both in that hee deliuered from him, and the rest of the Brethren.* And whereas furthermore in like sort, notice being giuen to the Ministers in prison, of one of *Copingers* fasts, it appeared not, what regard they had thereof: that point also is now cleared in the same Letter. *I beseech you also giue thankes, on my behalfe,*

Ibidem.

Ibidem.

behalfe, to the other eight preachers: for vpon notice giuen vnto them, by some of Gods children, that somewhat was intended to be don, wherein Gods Glory might appeare, and request made that the religious desires, and godly purposes of the faithful, might be strengthned by their holy praiers: they thereupon, (as it is credibly signified vnto me) humbled themselues in fasting and prayer: and such an extraordinary blessing came to me thereupon, as it is not fitte to be repeated. Ibidem.

Chap. IX.

Of Hackets first comming to Wigginton: of his gadding vp and downe: and of the designement to haue beene executed in the Star chamber.

EDmond *Copinger*, hauing thus proceeded in the course you haue heard of: at the length he did send againe for *Hacket*: the spirite (as it seemeth) mouing *Hacket*: before, to stay at home. Marry now, he straitghtly vrgeth him to be at *London*, *thre or foure daies, before the beginning of Trinity Terme: which hee could not be: but came vp the first day of the Terme which was the fourth of Iune 1591 and lodged at Islington.* The day following, he went to the Counter, and there dined with *Wigginton*: and after dinner, he beganne his Pageant, vz. to crie out against certaine of her Maiesties most honorable priuy Councell, and to vtter against them most villanous speches. The next day being *Sonday*, he wēt to haue heard maister *Phillippes preach*: but hee preached not that day there: as the Sexton informed him. Then *hee went*

Cop. to Hack.

Hackets discourse writen by Copinger.

4. Iune, 1591

to

to haue heard Maister Cooper: but seeing a Surples lie there, he departed thence, and went to Maister *Egertons* Sermon. At night, *not knowing where to lie, hee went to Wigginton: where he mette with Coppinger, and by Wiggintons appointment, hee lodged at Maister Lawsons.* The next morning, viz. the seuenth of *Iune*, he proceeded with his slanderous outcries against the said honorable Councellors: and so continued two dayes after. In the one of which two dayes, *hee was commaunded*, (as is sette downe) *to goe out of Paules by London gate, and say:* by your leaue London: *because hee knew, he was shortlie to remoue his dwelling.* The same day also, in the forenoone, he went to the Fleete, to haue spoken with Maister *Cartwright*: but missing of his purpose, hee left his message with the porter, vz. *that maister* Cartwright *should deale faithfullie in the Lords busines &c.* Of his afternoones worke, thus it is also in the same place recorded. *He was commaunded to sit that afternoone at maister* Lawsons *shoppe: but the purpose of the Lord in that, and what some of the Citizens themselues know,* (he saith) *I forbeare to speake.* These courses held by *Hacket*, in the streets, of exclaiming against such persons &c. did proceede (as it seemeth) by the aduise, or at least by the allowance of *Wigginton*. For it appeareth vnder his owne hand, that he approued (after his fashion) such outcries in the streetes to be lawfull, by two examples: *one out of* Iosephus, *and an other of a Yorkeshire man, that heretofore had vsed the like in London,* as *Wigginton recordeth.*

Ibidem.

About this tyme, vz. in *Iune*, (as I gesse,) one *Iohn Boman*, a seruant, in *Oundell*, did write thus to maister *Wigginton: I desire you to send me a Coppie of a writing, which you had from Maister Cartwright, vppon the Court matters, when Goodman Hacket was with you the first time.*

Boman to Wigginton. Iune. 1591.

Also, shortlie after the aforesaid outcries were finished,

and

and many other things thought vppon amongst them, (you may be sure to such seditious purposes:) the end of *Trinity* Tearme drew neare: when it was commonly expected, that *Cartwright* and the other ministers in prison, should haue come to their answere openly in the *Starre-chamber*. Whereupon a Letter was written, by *Copinger* to his most deare friend *Thomas Lancaster*, the Schoole-maister, from whom he could keepe nothing, that *Lancaster* in pollicy would suffer to be tould him. Which Letter *Lancaster* saith: he did teare in peeces, but confesseth vnder his hãd, that in the same these words were contained: vz. *If our Preachers in prison do appeare to morrow in the Star-chamber, and our great men deale with them so, as it is thought* 24. Iune. 1591 *they will: if God doe not throw some fearfull iudgement amongest them, so as some of the chiefe of them goe not aliue out of the place then neuer giue credite to me, in any thing, whilest you liue.* But maister *Cartwright* and the rest appeared not this day: and so the parties threatned, escaped this iudgement.

Chap. X.

A preparation towardes the intended disloialtie: two of Copingers Letters to Maister Charke: and to another: Cartwright and Wiggintons commendation of Penries being then in London.

NOt lõg after this time, (if not before) maister *Wiginton* and *Copinger*, were Wigg. ex. very busy, for the better preparing of the peoples mindes, to the readidier acceptation of their further purposes, to publishe in print two pamphlettes of *Wiggintons* pen-

penning, as he himselfe confesseth. The one was of Predestination, as though (by the abuse of that doctrine) they meant to haue had the blame of all the wicked and intended mischiefes, both of themselues and of their partakers, remoued from themselues, and layde vppon the Lordes shoulders: as though he should haue moued them to such lewd attemptes. The other was a kinde of *Ballade*, directed for aduice, to a yong courtier, wherein they make waye (as it seemeth) for their frend *Hacket*, and that with wonderfull quotation of Scriptures. I will trouble you onely with fowre of the verses.

A Christian true, although he be a clowne
May teach a King to weare Scepter and Crowne.

And after.

For God will sure confound such, as deuise
His ordinance or church to tirannise.

To these rimes, both for manner and matter, I may well resemble those, made (I doubt not) by the same spirit.

Epist. to Mart. Epitome.

Either from countrey or Court,
Martin Mar-Prelate will do you hurt.

Hack. decla.

Now that *Copinger* was a dealer in these thinges, with *Wiggintom* before they were printed, it appeareth by these wordes of *Hackets* in his last declaration to maister *Young*: *Wiggintons boy can declare all his Maisters writinges: for the boy and Maister Copinger, sate writing halfe a night, by this examinates bedde side, but what they writte, he cannot tell: but one word he heard:* that the Countrey Clowne, can teach the king to weare the Crowne.

After

Afterwardes (as I take it) viz. the 9. of *Iuly*, being fryday M. *Charke* preached at the blacke Fryers, at which Sermō *Copinger* was present: who missliking (as it seemeth) some wordes then vttered, did write a letter presently to M. *Charke*: wherein amongst other pointes, he sayth. *Right reuerend Sir &c. I do not denie (good Sir) but I haue now a long time taken a strange and extraordinary course, but such as hath offered occasion of suspition, of my not onely doing hurt to my selfe, but also to the best sort of men now in question, and to the cause it selfe. But by what warrant I haue done this, that is all. For if the holy Ghost hath beene my warrant, and carieth mee into such actions, as are differing from other mens &c. What flesh and blood dare speake against it, &c. Forbeare to censure me and such other, as should deale extraordinarily with mee, in the Lordes busines, committed to our charge, and iudge of vs, by the effectes which follow: which if you heareafter see to bee wonderderfull great, then let all ordinary men call themselues to an examination &c.* And after. *The waste of the Church cannot be denied to be greate, so that there is a place for extraordinary men, &c.* Againe, *my desire heretofore hath beene to haue hadde counsaile and direction: but now by comfortable experience, I finde, that the action which the Lorde hath drawn me into is his owne: and he will direct it himselfe by the holy Ghost &c*, To conclude, *I beseech you* (saith he) *to shew this letter to M. Trauers and M Egerton.* Cop. to Chark 9. Iuly. 1591.

M. Charke, vpon the receipt of this letter, preaching againe the *Sonday* after, in the same place, vttered in his sermon, these wordes, which (*Copinger* saith) were ment of him, in respect of his foresaide letter: *there are some persons so desperate that they would willingly thrust themselues vpon the rockes of the land.* This also appeareth by an other letter, cōcerning this second sermon, written about the 13. or 14 of *Iulie*, to an other preacher in *London*, but hee is not named Copin. to a preacher the 13. or 14. of *Iuly*.

med: it had beene to good purpose, if hee had beene named. For it seemeth hee was as throughly acquainted with *Coppinger*, and his fellowes designements, as it may be well supposed, that *Wigginton* was.

In my letter (vnto Charke) *I manifested my selfe to haue an extraordinarie calling, and signifyed, that the Lord had so called others besides my selfe, who would approue our selues, to bee the seruantes of the Lorde, in a high calling.* Againe *the ship* (that is the Church) *had perished, if the Lord had not immediately called three of vs, to helpe to recouer it* &c. *My calling is especially to deale with Magistrates: an other hath to doe with Ministers, who hath written a letter to you of the Citie &c. The thirde is the chiefe, who can neither write nor reade, so that hee is the executioner of the Lords most holy wil.* He further *offereth to acquaint this Minister, with their whole course, and willeth him to shew this letter to his brethren, and to publish it, where euer hee should goe.*

Hack. last ext. *Hacket* confessed, that being about this time, (as I take it) with *Wigginton*, the saide *Wigginton* affirmed, in the presence of two gentlemen and others, *that if the Magistrates did not gouerne well, the people might draw themselues together and to see a reformation.*

Vpon the 15. day of *Iuly*, *Copinger* and *Arthington* did write a iointe letter of purpose to haue drawne *Lancaster* vnto them, for the making vp of a quaternion. And this was one perswasion. *If I Ed. Coppinger, do not prefer you, before any one man in the land, whosoeuer, for your wise, holy, louing, and religious course, both in the generall calling of a Christian, and in your particular calling, the Lord confound me.*

After *Lancaster* had receiued this letter, notwithstanding he writ vnto him, of some mislike he had of their proceedings, yet (as *Hacket* saith,) *he came vnto them all three,*

the

the same night, to one Walkers house at Broken wharfe, where they conferred together about an hower after supper. Of what great account this *Lancaster* and some others were, with these companions, it doth further appeare by that which followeth. The same day in the morning that *Copinger* and *Arthington* made their seditious Proclamation in *Cheapside*: they two together first, and afterwarde *Hacket*, came vnto *Wigginton*, & amongst many things, (as *Wiginton* himselfe cōfesseth) they told him; that M. *Cartwright had done more against Antichrist then any in the worlde before him, since the Apostles times; and that Wigginton, was comparable vnto him, and that M. Lancaster was aboue them both, in the estate of heauenlie glorie, because he had kept himselfe vndefiled from the common corruptions of these times, and had a most simple hart to God.* Likewise also they saide to *Wigginton*, at the same time, that *Reformation and the Lordes discipline should now forthwith bee established: and therefore charged Wigginton in the Lordes name to put all Christians in comfort, that they should see a ioyfull alteration, in the state of Church gouernment, shortly.*

Hack.ex. 21 of Iuly.

16, of Iuly

Arthington, after being examined said, that *Penry* had sent him word by a letter out of *Scotland*, *that reformation must shortlie be erected in England: and that he tooke him (in so writing) to bee a true Prophet.* It is not also vnlikely, but that *Penry* was a Prouoker of these men to such their outrages: hoping, that vpon their outcries & proclamations the people would haue risen. For *he was then in London* to haue played his part if their attempts had found the good successe, they looked for. Marry when he saw *Hacket* executed: he presentlie (the same day) posted backe againe towards *Scotland*.

Ienk. Ioh. ex

Chap. XI.

Of the trayterous intendments which were towardes the Court.

BEfore this their intended insurrection, it is to be further remembrd vnto you what was disclosed amongst themselues in their owne discourses and prophesies,(as since it appeareth,)cōcerning the meanes, whereby they thought to haue preuailed, for their discipline, &c. by those their most lewde, seditious, and trayterous attempts. Her Maiesties course helde, for the maintenance of the present gouernement of the Church: was their chiefe grief,(which course they tearmed *the defence of abhomination: the bearing of the beasts marke, the thrusting of Iesus Christ out of his own rule & gouernment) and the arraignement of some, with the imprisonment of Cartwright & others.*

Arthingtons prophesie.

Vdall. &c.

If the *Starre chamber* day (before mentioned) had held some of her Maiesties most honourable priuy Counsaile, (whom they supposed to stand most in their light) should neuer haue departed thence aliue. After that plot fayling they deuised how by their imprecations and cursing of themselues they might perswade the people, that certaine of the Lordes of the saide most *honourable Counsaile*, were traytors. Wherein how they preuailed I know not: but this I find, that they had not onely *determined to haue remoued them all from her Maiestie*: & to haue *placed others in their roomes*, (whom they had already named particularly,) but likewise to haue proceeded against their LL^s. with very hard censures. *The Lord pardon their soules*, (saith *Copinger*) *for in their*

Coppinger in a letter.

their outward man, they must be punished, though they repent. Nay in their own conceits: they had likewise already depriued some of the chiefe of their LL[s] from their greate places of honor: so as when they tooke occasion, to speake seditiously of them, they vsed their bare names, without any of the honourable titles, belonging vnto them: as such a man *lately such an officer, Chancellor or Treasurer, &c.*

Besides (when the time of their said intended insurrection grew nigh,) they sent to haue her Maiestie moued for the committing of her saide Councellors: least in the vprores, which they meant to stir, their LL[s]. might haue beene violently surprised &c. they hauing peraduenture some purpose, to bring them afterwardes to some of their own more publike courtes of iustice. *I do aduise* (saith *Coppinger,*) *that euery one of her Councell, be commanded, to keepe their house or chamber for feare of stir & danger: and that such and such, &c. be appointed to waite vpon her: and that maister* Wigginton, (*in more fauour with God then any man of his calling, whosoeuer,*) *be commanded to be neare her* highnesse, *to pray to God, and to preach priuately, &c.* Ibid.

But that which is especially most horrible, (although they might seem, by this last prouision, for her Maiesty, to haue indeede some good regard of her safety) yet is it cōfessed to haue bin affirmed amongst them: *that her highnes was worthy to be depriued, for giuing credite and countenance to the Bishops and such other wicked persons: and for misusing her good subiectes,* I think they ment the imprisonment of *Cartwright* and the rest. Arthin. exam. 19. of Iuly

It is also further confessed by *Arthington,* that his fellowes *refused to pray for her Maiestie:* and in his second examination, he acknowledgeth, that *hee verily thinketh, that Hacket meant her Maiestie should haue beene depriued:* and in his long *Apologie* vnto the LL[s]. thus: *In my conscience Hacket*

ket meant to murther those noble men, that hindered his purpose, one way or other, &c. and after, &c, to haue done that, which my heart and hand for trembling cannot expresse.

Agreeable hereunto, are *Hackets* wordes, both before he was condemned, and after. *If* (saith he) Copinger, *one* Catiline *late of* Oundell, *&* Wigginton *were straitly examined: they could vtter and declare matters of treason.* And at an other time: *If these fellowes* (meaning *Copinger* and *Wigginton, &c*) *were wel sifted, they could declare al the treasons.* And the morning before his death. *It was a gratious and an happie turne, that these treasons were in time reuealed: for otherwise it would haue cost a number of innocent men their bloud: but now (I trust in God,) that they will reueale their treasons.* And thus you see the end and drift of the foresaid *extraordinary* callings, for the setting vp and establishing of the pretended holy discipline.

Hack. on the torture.

Hacket examined. 24. Iuly

Hacket to M. Yong in presence of diuerse.

Chap. XII.

That of long time, some such attemptes as Hacket made for Discipline: were of greate likelyhood purposed.

Conspiracy for Discipline

MY purpose was not, from the beginninge, eyther to set downe, or to prosecute, the full hystorie of these desperate reformers, (which is most effectually performed already by another), otherwise then they doe concerne some other persons, and especially those, not of the meanest of our *Disciplinarian* Ministers, and are therby verie pertinent (in my opinion) to shew the point, I haue in hand, of the brethrens imitation of the *Scottish* ministers reformation. For I trust (as I said, in the entrance to this part,) it wil not now be denied but that great & many threatning speaches are published.

One

One telleth vs, *that great troubles will come of it, if the brethren may not be suffered* to do what they list: another, *that they can no longer endure to bee vsed as they are*: another in effect: *that our Bishops shalbe vsed, as they were in Scotland*: and that there *are moe* of this confederacy, *then can be suppressed*: another, *that it is more then time, for the hottest brethren to set vp the Discipline themselues, without any further staying for Parliaments*: a Synode, *that the people, being first instructed, are then to bee thrust into the publike practise of the Discipline*: another man, *that seeing the brethren cannot obtain their wils, by sute nor dispute, the multitude and people must worke the feat*: another, *that inferior Magistrates of their owne authority, within their limits, are to make this new reformation*: another, *that it is a shame for all the fauorers of this faction, in that for feare of disturbing of our state, (forsooth,) and offending of her Maiestie, they had not before this time cast out our Bishops*: another, *that there are a hundred thousand of this brotherhoode in England, who if they come with a petition for the discipline to her Maiestie, cannot in pollicie be reiected, without danger*: another *that approoued and worthy men of euerie shire haue already consented to this Discipline: that the Eldership is at hande*: that *the people are inflamed with zeale, & that it is impossible to stand against it*: another, *that there is a deuise amongst them, how to obteine their desires all in one day*: another, *that Bishops are to be packing after the Fryers and Monkes*: another, *that they will haue their Discipline in spight of all the aduersaries of it*: another, *that it is dangerous to the state, if they haue not their willes, in regard of the discontentment, which wil ensue thereby, in the heartes of her Maiesties subiectes*: another *in* effect, *that the Discipline is like to come into our Church, by such a meanes, as will make all the Bishoppes heartes to ake*: and another, *that he is of this minde, that reformation wil not be had without bloud.*

Now if any man, to extenuate these things, shal say: let euery man beare his own burthen, & be charged with his own particular actions: what some in the heate of their zeale haue published, it ought to haue a charitable construction, & cannot wel be further extended, to touch any other: as if al the factioners had entred into such a seditious conspiracie, as the said threatning speeches do import, I answere, that some indeede there be, that do cast these & such like colours ouer this matter, to bleare mens eyes withall. Some commends their zeale, but not their discretion: some allow their matter, but not their manner: and some will take vpon them to excuse both: but as yet I neuer heard any of that crue, but hee would eyther in one respect or other, find some occasion to commend the worst of them.

Besides where so many of any one sect do concurre in their writings, about any new point: it is commonly taken to be the iudgement of them all. And who knoweth not, that if *Cartwright* and the rest, had not secretly clapped such fellowes on the backs for their zeale, and laughed in their sleeues to see them go so forward, but had disliked them: his earnest reproofe of the first (being their *Apostle* and *worthy*) would haue preuented all the others that followed, being his *Disciples.* But if it be true, (that I haue heard reported) that vpon the comming forth of *Martins* Epistle: *Maister Cartwright* should say: *seeing the Bishops would take no warning: it is no matter that they are thus handled:* Surely those words, from him were enough to set these men agogge. So as, that which is commonly reported of great robberies: may fitly serue to satissie the bowlsterers of such lewdnesse.

There are (say they) in such attemptes not onely executioners, but also setters, receiuers, and fauourers: and in matters

matters of treason concealers : who are all of them within the daunger & compasse of law. How this may be applied, I leaue it, to any reasonable mans consideration, that shall be pleased to weigh the premisses, aswell concerning the said threatning speaches & great bragges: as also the course which was helde, by the ministers in prison, and those of the *London-fraternitie*, together with some others, touching the attemptes, which *Coppinger* and his fellowes tooke vpon them to effect.

CHA. XIII.

Briefe collections: whereby it may summarily appeare: that certaine Ministers in London did know, what Coppinger intended.

Igginton (as you haue heard) vpon *Cartwrightes* commitment, &c. writeth *of a bickering, and then a battell to be looked for. Coppinger* with his companiõs *fasteth, &* so dreameth of a way, howe to worke wonders. He sendeth *into Scotland concerning an extraordinary calling, signifying that some did fancy to themselues such a manner of calling, who would hazard their liues, that Christ himselfe, by the abolishing of the Antichristian tyranny,* (which he affirmed did raigne in our Church,) *might gouerne in his owne kingdome. Wigginton* afterwarde *approueth the lawfulnesse of such a calling, in these dayes, our Churches lying wast &c. Copinger* and *Wigginton* with some others, *do thereupon fast againe, to know which of them should be so called.* The lot (forsooth) falling vpon *Copinger chiefly* he is not silent: but maister *Wentworth* (amongst others)

 must

must be of his priuy Councel. He also disclosed himselfe, (after a sort) as you haue heard, *to certaine of the Ministers in London* before mentioned: and namely *to Maister Cartwright, imparting vnto him his seuerall callings to an extraordinary course for the discipline, &c. His said writings into Scotland*, and *Wiggintons said approbation of an extraordinary calling*. He sent *Maister Cartwright the same propositions, that Wigginton had allowed:* whereof maister *Cartwright, afterwardes thought, there might bee good vse :* hee signified vnto him, *that by his calling, he was to take in hand such busines, as in the eyes of flesh and bloud, was likely to bring great danger to himselfe, and vnlikely to bring any good successe to the Church:* he told him, *that if he had not beene discouraged, he had before that day procured the release of some, that stoode then in daunger of their liues*, meaning (as I suppose) *Vdall*, and *Newman, &c.*

As he dealt with *Cartwright*, so did he with the other Ministers, and with some of them more plainely, desiring still of them all, both *Cartwright and the rest, and that most instantlie, that he might be conferred withall, offering himselfe to be altogether ruled by them, either to proceede (if they thought meete) in his saide so dangerous businesse, or otherwise wholy to desist and leaue it off*. He also offered to imparte *vnto them all his designements, as to M. Cartwright*, not onely *in generality what he intended, but also the particular meanes, whereby he purposed to bring the same to passe.* Afterwardes when through his acquaintance with *Hacket*, by *Wiggintons* meanes, & other incouragements giuen him by *an other of his lay friendes*: and by *Wigginton &c*, that he grew to be more resolute : hee signifyed the same to *M. Charke*, (not past six days before their furie brake forth,) stil *yet desiring conference* with him, *Trauers, Egerton, Gardiner, Cooper and Philips.*

CHAP

CHAP. XIIII.

The cunning dealing of certaine ministers in London, how notwithstanding they wished Coppingers plot to goe forward: yet they might be (if it were possible) without the compasse of law.

Onsider I pray you the policy, which the saide ministers (mentioned in the end of the former Chap.) vsed. They at the beginning, no sooner heard of *Copingers* conceit of an extraordinary calling, to worke such great matters: but by & by, (as mē acquainted with the fore-saide *Geneua* positions,) they very well knewe, wherunto that matter tended. And therefore wher-as the poore misse-led gentleman, would haue imparted vnto them, al his secretes: they started from that point, and refused wholy to take from him any knowledge of them.

They sent him some cold messages, of their dislike of his proceedings, (which they after qualified, as it hath been shewed,) not so much to with-draw him from his lewdenesse, as that therby if thinges fell out amisse, they might haue some meanes to cleare themselues, by the testimonies of such their messengers, as *Hockenhull* and others. And touching conference that was also by them denied, and surely vpon good and prouident reasons. For if therby, they shou ld haue yelded in opinion vnto him, they knewe it might haue broughr them into apparant danger. Besides, they were not vnlike by sufficient arguments to haue disswaded him, from such a fantasie: which (as it seemeth) was very farre from their meaning. And lastly, it was almost impossible, but that in their debating with him of his pretended calling, he must needes haue made some mention of such particulars, as with their own safety they durst not haue concealed: & so that way also his platforme would haue beene dashed. The safest way therefore, for them was, not to haue any conference at all with him: and that course (for ought I finde) they tooke: to the hardning of *Coppingers* hart, and his fellowes: and to the greate aduenturing of all the mischiefes, that were intended.

It was not denied amongst them, (as *Coppinger* sayth,) *but that the cause was good, which he desired to be an actor in: but the thing that stucke* in their teeth, was this: vz. *they thought it impossible that he should be fit to intermeddle in it, without the endaungering both of himselfe* (as Egerton saide,) *and of the greate cause which hee would seeme to bee most desirous to further*. Howbeit though *Egerton* would not take vpon him, to approue his *extraordinarie* calling, (for feare of him-selfe :) yet (for all the saide daunger) hee thought it no pollicy greatly to discourage him, when he qualified his speeches after this sort: vz. *hee would bee loth to quench the spirite of God in Coppinger, or to hinder his zeale.*

Numb.27. Deut.31 *Iosuah* was called *extraordinarily* by God him-selfe, to cast the enemies of the *Israelites* out of the land of *Canaan*,
Iosuah.1.9. that they might possesse it. Which example *M. Wentworth* applying to *Coppinger*, and encouraging him, vpon aduice taken, as the Lord did *Iosuah* : vz : *be bold & of a good courage, feare not to bee discouraged &c.* he shewed no greate mislike of *Copingers* purposes. Likewise, though *M. Throgmorton*, notwithstãding his cõference, (as it seemeth) with *Coppinger, Arthington* and *Hacket*, was not acquainted (as he saide,) with *Copingers* particular platformes: yet in that he confesseth, *he had heard some buzzes abroade of a*

sole

sole and singular course intended, & doth not only *aduise him to imitate the serpentes wisedome*, but saith also, *that in affection and good will he ioyned with him:* :it could not otherwise be, but that *Coppinger* was thereby greatly animated.

When *Copinger* tolde *Vdall* that certaine *vnlearned men, then lyinge hid, would shortlie take vpon them the defence of the cause, which hee and his brethren in prison stood-for, and woulde thereby daunt all their ennemies, more then they coulde*, willinge *both him and the rest, ther-vpon to cheare vp themselues,* (*for the day of their redemption was at hand:* I doe greately maruaile, what *Vdall* thought to bee *Copingers* meaning.

It might well haue stoode with *M. Charkes* duety, (seeing *Coppingers* full resolution to enter into some desperate attempt, by vertue of his extraordinarie calling,) to haue disclosed the same to the state. When he preached in the *Blacke-Friers*, to the brotherhood there, about two days after his said intelligence of *Copingers* resolution, and but fiue or six daies before their proclamation that *there were some persons, so desperate that they would willinglie thrust themselues vpon the rockes of the Land*; thereby to haue disswaded *Copinger*, (who then was present,) or for what other purpose, *I* know not: hee should forth with haue acquainted the saide rockes also, what boisterous tempestes and violẽt stormes had beene ready to assault them.

In this briefe summary, I omitte the rest of *Wiggintons* actions, referring you to his fellow *Hackets* iudgement, both of him and them. They are so apparant, by that which hath been sayd, as they seeme to me, to be past coniectures. And I would withal my hart, that all which hath bene hetherto saide of the other ministers, touching this pointe, did onely depende vpon probabilities. For then charity would binde vs to iudge the best. But men may not cal *good euill, nor darkenesse light*, nor treasonable conspiracies, ecclesiasticall pollicies. Marke them (if it please you) for *disciplinarian practises* : and then bearing that brande, owne them, who liste, and tearme them as you fancy.

Chap. XV.

If Hackets treasons had preuailed for the pretended discipline, how they might haue beene defended by the disciplinarie doctrine.

Am not ignorant, that now, if any of the saide ministers or their fauorers were asked, how they like of *Coppingers* and his companions proceedings: no men will more eagerlie exclaime against them. When *Hacket* with his adherents, found themselues preuented, and that they were cut of in the beginning of their race, then (to saue their liues) they could confes, their extraordinary purposes, pretended before with teares, with fasting, (with grones and imprecations, to haue proceeded from the spirit of God,) to be nothing else, but illusions of Sathã, cruel, bloody, & trayterous designements. But if they had preuailed, what would haue been said of them then? Surely it is no hard matter to gesse. If *Coppinger, Hacket*, and *Arthington*, had murthered two or three of the Lords in the *Star-chamber*, the last day of the said *Trinity Terme*, the *Consistorian* doctrine would easily haue defended it: especially if their further intents for the discipline, had thereby succeeded. I will tell you a notable historie to this purpose.

About the yeare 1545. (M. *Caluin* then raigning in the

Con-

Consistorie at *Geneua*,) one *Norman Lesly* son to the *Earle of Rothsey*, fell at some iarre with the *Archbishop of S. Andrewes*, then a *Cardinall*: for a *priuate cause* (saith our *Chronicle* & *Buchanans*) betwixt them two, for his dealing, concerning the burning *of one George Wisehart*, (saith the history of the Church of *Scotland*.) Whereupon the said *Normã*, with some of his *partakers conspired the Cardinals death*, they being the rather animated therunto, *throgh the Councell of some greate men of the Realme, that had conceiued some deadly hatred against him.* The effecting of which conspiracie, proceeded after this sort, as is set downe in the saide *Ecclesiasticall history*. The 29. of Maie *1546*, the saide *Norman*, with *16*, or *17*. moe, entred by a wile into the Castle of *S. Andrewes*, (where the *Cardinal* dwelt) early in the morning: and after some course taken for possessing themselues of the castle, *Norman Lesly, Iames Meluin, and Peter Carmichaell*, got into the *Cardinals* chamber, where finding him set in his chayre, and crying vnto them: *I am a Priest, yee will not slay mee? the saide Leesly stroke him first, once or twise, and so did the saide Peter. But Iames Meluin (a man, you may be sure, of nature most gentle and most modest,) perceiuing them both in choller, withdrew them, and saide: This worke and iudgement of God, (although it be secrete,) ought to be done with greater grauitie. And presenting vnto him the point of the sworde, saide. Repent thee of thy former wicked life, but especially of the shedding of the blood, of that notable instrument of God, M. George Wisehart, which albeit the flame of fire consumed before men, yet cries it a vengeance vpon thee, and we from God are sent to reuenge it. For here before my God, I protest that neither the hatred of thy person, the loue of thy riches, nor the feare of any trouble, thou couldest haue done to mee in particular, moued, or moueth me to strike thee: but onely because thou hast beene and remainest an obstinate enemie against*

The hist. of the church of Scotland. pa. 143. 144. 145.

F. Thyn. and Buchanan.

Hist. of the church of Scotland.

The godly fact and wordes of Iam. Meluin.

 Christ

Christ Iesus and his holy Gospell. And so hee stroke him, twise or thrise through, with a stog-sworde : and so he fell. The *Cardinall* being thus murthered, *they seized vpon the Artillerie and munition, wherewith that fortresse was plentifully furnished, and likewise vpon the rich hangings, householde stuffe, of all sortes, apparell, Copes, iewels, ornamentes of Churches, greate store of gold and siluer plate, besides no small quantitie of treasure in ready coine.*

F. Thin. and Buchanan.

Some amongst vs in *Englande*, haue laboured very earnestlie to qualifie *Copingers* words, where he said, *that God would throw some fearefull iudgement amongst the Lordes, so as some the chiefe of them should not goe aliue out of the place* : as though there had beene no violent course intended by him & his associates, but that (in his fond conceit (he had imagined, that God himselfe from heauen, should haue shewed that iudgement, for the deliuerance of *Cartwright* and the rest. And in my conscience, one gentelman of good credit, not acquainted at all with the *Consistorian* doctrine, in these & such like matters thought so in his hart. But here this maske is pluckt from such faces as could not be ignorant, what was ment, in that the same spirit which Was in *Copinger*, speaking before in *Iames Meluin*, or rather (as I thinke) in *Knox*, and his fellow-ministers, (according to whose humor he penned that history,) doe tearme the saide cruell murther of the *Cardinall*, to bee the *worke and iudgement of God*, & that for the manner of the executiō of it. Besides in the margent of the Booke: ouer against the Stabbers blasphemous wordes, this note is set downe, vz. *the godly fact and wordes of Iames Meluin.* But that, which mooueth me most, and for the which I haue troubled you with this historie, is this : that men are animated to commit the like murthers, and the doctrine thereof is stoutely iustified according to the heathenish conceit, of a certaine

tyrant

tyrant, whom *Cicero* also (a heathen man, but yet of better iudgement) doth confute.

Dionisius, hauing spoiled the temple of *Proserpina*, at *Locris*, of *Iupiter* in *Peloponesus*, of *Aesculapius* at *Epidaurus*, because *Proserpina* drowned him not, as he sayled to *Syracuse* nor *Iupiter* stroke him in peeces with his thunderboltes, nor *Aesculapius* made an ende of him by some long & miserable consumption, both he himselfe, and many others, accounted such his sacrilege, to be both iust and lawfull. And euen so it falleth out, for the murther I speake of. He that hath eyes to see let him see.

Cicer. de natura deorum lib. 3.

After the foresaid Castel was surprised, and the *Cardinall* was murthered, *Lesly* with his company, *Knox* and the rest kept the same Castel by force against the Gouernor. But at the last they were compelled to yeeld it vp: and being thereupon sent (as prisonners) into *Fraunce*, they were (by directions there) committed some of thẽ to the Gallies, and some to other prisons. Howbeit in the ende they all escaped with their liues, by one meanes or other, sauing the saide *Iames Meluin*, who dyed in prison, whereupon commeth in this notable *Consistorian* doctrine, borrowed of the said heathenish conclusions.

The hist. of the church Scotland.

This we write, vz. (how all but *Meluin* escaped) *to let the posterities to come vnderstand*, (saith *Knox* and his fellowes) *how potently God wrought, in preseruing and deliuering of these that had but a smal knowledge of his truth, & for the loue of the same hazarded all. That if that, eyther we (now in our dayes,) hauing greater light, or our posterities, (that shall follow vs) shal see a fearefull dispersion of such as oppone themselues to impiety, or take vpon them to punish the same, otherwise then lawes of men will permit: if (wee say) we or they shall see such left of men yea as it were despised and punished of God, yet let vs not damne the persons that punish vice. (and that for iust cause:) nor yet de-*

spaire, but that the same God, that deiects (for causes vnknowen to vs) will raise vp againe the persons deiected to his glorie, and their comfort.

Againe if our said seditious persons had preuailed with the multitude, (in their other plot) concerning their purposes of remouing some of her maiesties most honorable *Priuy Councell*, from her seruice in that place: and in appointing others to succeede them, (whom they fancied to be fauourers of their Discipline): you should haue heard (I warrant you) no cries of the brotherhood, nor complaints in your streets, of any of that faction. It would haue beene saide, as *Goodman* taught at *Geneua*, that seeing the saide *Councellors were enemies to Christes kingdome, and did seduce her Maiestie now, that God had raised them vp, an* Othoniel *or a* Ionathan *to assist them*, why should they not haue ioyned themselues vnto him? Oh (would some haue said) *the holy discipline, the holy discipline, the holy discipline: what Prince or Potentate may resist the holy discipline and prosper?* Others. *See the hand of the Lorde: when men do faile what God can doe.* Others, *the greatest workes, that euer were done in the behalfe of the Church, haue beene brought to passe by the basest meanes.* Others, *this is the worke of God, and it is admirable in our eyes.* Others, *thus* Iosuah *being extraordinarily strengthned by God, threw thirty kings out of the land of Canaan.* Others, *sufficient warning was giuen, & what would they haue had men to haue done?* Then should you haue had such a declaration, or proclamation, as you haue before heard of: penned (no doubt) by some of the *Consistorian ministers in Scotlād:* vz. *of the iust and necessary causes, mouing them and their assistantes her Maiesties faithfull subiects, to repaire to her Maiesty: for resisting of the present daungers, appearing to Gods true religion and professors thereof, &c. and to seeke redres and reformation of abuses, remouing from her Maiesty, the chiefe authors therof*

Declaration 1582, before mentioned.

of &c. that with common consent, redresse and remedy might bee prouided: Or termed. *The repairing towards Greenwitch to the Q. Maiesty*, as else where such attempts haue been colored. Proclamation at Sterling. 1585. F. Thin.

Likewise, if yet thinges had not squared to their likings, and that they had gone further with good successe in any violent course against her maiesty, (as it is confessed they purposed to haue done,) then also the *Geneua-diuinity* must haue borne the brunt, for the iustification of such extraordinary iudgementes of God. And thus you should haue had these matters smoothed ouer, as partly it may appeare by the assault mentioned at *Sterling*, wherein the king was present in person: and partly by the *Consistorian* propositions, (before set down) touching this point, with many other things, both to be noted in the premises, and also in those bookes, out of the which the saide propositions are drawen.

I will not trouble you any further with *Ifs*, although I could adde, that if the said traitors had proceeded on forward, with their confessed purposes, to haue touched her maisties estate: there wanteth no lesse defence, by *Disciplinarian* learning, for such a matter, then for the premises. You may remember the seditious & intollerable propositions before mentioned, as they are truely collected out of our own countrey mens books, infected at *Geneua* with that pestilent doctrine. Many examples also would haue beene brought, for that purpose, out of *Buchanan, Beza, Knox* and the rest of that humor: especiallie the graue resolution giuen by *Knox* and *Wollocke*, generally against all Princes, but particularly then vrged and effected, by the deposing of the king of *Scots* grandmother, from her ciuil gouernment of that land. And peraduenture a part of the said *Knox* his exhortation to *England* written from *Geneua* the twelfth of *Ianuary* 1559. (as soone as he hearde of her Histo. of the Church of Scotland, pa. 372 373. Exhort pag. 91. 92.

 maiesties

maiesties possession of the royall Crown of this Realme,) would haue beene iustified: where he saith, that *no power, nor liberty, ought to be permitted to any state, degree, or authority, (whatsoeuer they bee:) to liue without the yoke of Discipline, &c: and that if Prince, King or Emperour, would enterprise to change or disanull the same, he ought to be reputed an ennemie to God, and therefore vnworthy to raigne aboue his people.*

And thus you see how al these treasons, if they had happened, with what *Consistorian* zeale they might haue been defended afterward, by the *Disciplinarian* doctrine, which hath beene sent abroade into this *Iland* from *Geneua*: and meetely well practised already, in some partes thereof, by men of that stampe. Whereupon I do collect, (the premisses considered) by *Cartwrights* & other the ministers intelligence, with *Copingers* desperate purposes, that they cared not what mischiefs had ensued, so they themselues might haue beene safe. For (as it is most euident, by the threatning speeches before mentioned,) there is nothing more laboured for, amongst that sect, then to thrust their many thousandes, or some of them into some mutiny or bloudy attempt. Their hope was, that vpon any such occasion, their chiefe fauourers would not cease to solicit her maiesty, (for feare of further trouble) to graunt their desires, or (at the least) to take some other course, for theyr contentment, then hitherto (in their opinions) there hath beene taken. They knew, that whatsoeuer either could or should fal out, vnder the pretẽce of seeking for Christs kingdome, and for the extirpation of the present gouernment of our Church (tearmed by them to bee so *abhominable & Antichristian*,) if it had good successe for their deuised platformes, yet the said *Consistorian* examples, with their *Allobrogicall* new learning, would haue borne it out sufficiently and maintained it. I pray God deliuer *Englãd* from

from these and such like points of *Discipline.*

For mine own part, I would not haue, vrged matters in this sort, were it not, that I thinke (in my conscience) it is more then high time, that her maiesties faithfull subiectes should learne to know these practises, and withall to beware of such sectaries, as (vnder their many, both godly and goodly pretences) do thus seditiously endeuour to disturbe the land. And the rather also, I did it, because I see there are diuerse, that will needes hood-winke themselues, and stop their eares, with the Serpent in the *Psalme* of purpose, because they would gladly haue these things smoothered vp. For hereby it will be apparant to our posterity, that if any such mischiefes, (which God forbid) shal happen hereafter, they were sufficiently warned, that both should and might (in good time) haue preuented them, and withall it would then be found true which *Liuie* saith: *vrgentibus rempublicam fatis, Dei & hominum salutares admonitiones spernuntur.* When the Lorde for the sinnes of the people, is purposed to punish any Countrey: he blindeth the eyes of the wise, so as they shall either neglect, or not perceiue those ordinary meanes, for the safety thereof, which very simple men, (or babes in a manner) did easily foresee. Which iudgement I pray God turne far away, and long from this and all other true Christian lands and kingdomes. Amen.

Lib. 5 dec. 1

FINIS.

Date Due